# THE REFORM OF LEGAL PROCEDURE

Published @ 2017 Trieste Publishing Pty Ltd

ISBN 9780649688333

The Reform of Legal Procedure by Moorfield Storey

Except for use in any review, the reproduction or utilisation of this work in whole or in part in any form by any electronic, mechanical or other means, now known or hereafter invented, including xerography, photocopying and recording, or in any information storage or retrieval system, is forbidden without the permission of the publisher, Trieste Publishing Pty Ltd, PO Box 1576 Collingwood, Victoria 3066 Australia.

All rights reserved.

Edited by Trieste Publishing Pty Ltd.
Cover @ 2017

This book is sold subject to the condition that it shall not, by way of trade or otherwise, be lent, re-sold, hired out, or otherwise circulated without the publisher's prior consent in any form or binding or cover other than that in which it is published and without a similar condition including this condition being imposed on the subsequent purchaser.

www.triestepublishing.com

# MOORFIELD STOREY

# THE REFORM OF LEGAL PROCEDURE

# THE REFORM OF
# LEGAL PROCEDURE

BY
MOORFIELD STOREY

NEW HAVEN: YALE UNIVERSITY PRESS
LONDON: HENRY FROWDE
OXFORD UNIVERSITY PRESS
MCMXI

COPYRIGHT, 1911,
BY YALE UNIVERSITY PRESS

First printed September, 1911, 750 copies

THE ADDRESSES CONTAINED IN THIS BOOK WERE
DELIVERED IN THE WILLIAM L. STORRS LECTURE
SERIES, 1911, BEFORE THE LAW SCHOOL OF YALE
UNIVERSITY, NEW HAVEN, CONNECTICUT

# CONTENTS

| | | PAGE |
|---|---|---|
| I | THE CONDITIONS OF THE PROBLEM AND THE RESPONSIBILITIES OF THE LAWYER . . . . . . . . | 1 |
| II | THE REDUCTION OF LITIGATION BY LEGISLATION . . . . . . . . . . | 50 |
| III | DELAYS DURING TRIAL . . . . . | 91 |
| IV | DELAY IN APPELLATE COURTS . . | 145 |
| V | CRIMINAL PROCEDURE. THE LAWYER'S RESPONSIBILITIES FOR LEGISLATION . . . . . . . . . . . | 193 |

# THE REFORM OF LEGAL PROCEDURE

# THE REFORM OF LEGAL PROCEDURE

## I

### THE CONDITIONS OF THE PROBLEM AND THE RESPONSIBILITIES OF THE LAWYER

"THE corner-stone of this republic, as of all free governments, is respect for and obedience to the law."

These words of Theodore Roosevelt state a political axiom which every citizen is bound to uphold. No one has stated this obligation more strongly than Abraham Lincoln when he said:

"Let reverence for the law be breathed by every American mother to the babe that prattles on her lap; let it be taught in schools and colleges; let it be preached from the pulpit, proclaimed in legislative halls and enforced in courts of justice. And, in short, let it become the political religion of the nation, and let the old and the young, the rich and the poor, the grave and the gay, of all sexes and tongues and colors and conditions, sacrifice unceasingly upon its altars."

This duty of every citizen is peculiarly the duty of the lawyer. We cannot respect ourselves unless we respect the law whose guardians we are, and every man who enters the Bar assumes thereby an obligation to make the law, its precepts and its practice, worthy of respect. This is his first and last debt to his profession. The great lawyers of the past have been the leaders of the community, and have deserved and enjoyed in ample measure the confidence of their fellow-citizens. To-day unhappily, for reasons which I shall discuss later, the law and its ministers are no longer trusted as implicitly, but on the contrary are attacked from every side, and lawlessness increases the country over.

For example, let me quote the language of President Taft, whose long and varied experience at the Bar, on the Bench, and in the most exacting administrative office qualifies him peculiarly to

## CONDITIONS OF THE PROBLEM

speak, and whose authority certainly will not be questioned here. Speaking at Chicago, in September, 1909, he said:

"There is no subject upon which I feel so deeply as upon the necessity for reform in the administration of both civil and criminal law. To sum it all up in one phrase, the difficulty in both is undue delay. It is not too much to say that the administration of criminal law in this country is a disgrace to our civilization, and that the prevalence of crime and fraud, which here is greatly in excess of that in the European countries, is due largely to the failure of the law and its administration to bring criminals to justice. I am sure that this failure is not due to corruption of officials. It is not due to their negligence or laziness, though of course there may be both in some cases; but it is chiefly due to the system against which it is impossible for an earnest prosecutor and an efficient judge to struggle.

. . . . . .

But reform in our criminal procedure is not the

only reform that we ought to have in our courts. On the civil side of the courts there is undue delay, and this always works for the benefit of the man with the longest purse. The employment of lawyers and the payment of costs all become more expensive as the litigation is extended. It used to be thought that a system by which cases involving small amounts could be carried to the Supreme Court through two or three courts of intermediate appeal was a perfect system, because it gave the poor man the same right to go to the Supreme Court as a rich man. Nothing is further from the truth. What the poor man needs is a prompt decision of his case; and by limiting the appeals in cases involving small amounts of money, so that there shall be a final decision in the lower court, an opportunity is given to the poor litigant to secure a judgment in time to enjoy it, and not after he has exhausted all his resources in litigating to the Supreme Court.

. . . . . . .

CONDITIONS OF THE PROBLEM

Of all the questions that are before the American people, I regard no one as more important than this, to wit: The improvement of the administration of justice."

Another accuser is your own teacher, Professor Vance, who, when Dean of the George Washington University, said:

"Bluntly put, the American lawyer has proved a failure. In no other free and civilized country are the laws so ill-administered as in these United States. We lead the world in most of the great struggles mankind is making, but in the administration of the law America lags two generations behind the rest of the civilized world. No constructive reforms of a comprehensive kind have been seriously attempted since the days of David Dudley Field, now passed a half century and more. Our inefficient procedure in civil actions is a reproach to the nation and a disgrace to the bar, while our procedure in criminal cases, with its enormous expense, its incredible delays, and its frequent and gross mis-carriages of justice, is a stench in the nostrils of the nations.

The legal profession in America is blighted by two serious faults. The first is a low moral tone, manifesting itself, in its worst form, in deliberate preying upon the public, legal parasitism, and, in its less repulsive form, in a selfish indifference to the deep public interest with which the calling of the lawyer is affected. The second is a lack of knowledge of the law as a science, as distinguished from knowledge of the law as a craft."

These are criticisms of the Bar, but the Bench is not spared. You will recall the severe censure with which Judge Humphreys and other judges were visited some years ago by our last President, because their decisions did not accord with his views, and his attacks during the recent political campaign upon the Supreme Court of the United States and upon other eminent judges, whom he characterized variously as "fossilized," "reactionary," or in even less flattering terms. Whatever we may think of such language, it cannot be

## CONDITIONS OF THE PROBLEM

ignored, for it at once expresses and creates a popular distrust of our judiciary at a time when it is dealing with the most vital questions and the most powerful interests in the country, when it is asked at once to restrain the aggressions of capital and the excesses of labor, and when, therefore, it needs, as perhaps never before, the full confidence and ungrudging support of the public.

This loss of confidence in the courts finds expression, not only in political harangues, but in legislation, like the law recently passed in Massachusetts, which takes from the courts the power to punish for contempt where the act punished is a crime, unless the accused is first convicted by a jury; and the provision in the new constitution of Arizona, which makes it possible to recall a judge if his decisions are unpopular. I shall give you other examples of this tendency, but these are enough for my present purpose, taken as they are from the oldest and the newest states of the union.

A very significant expression of popular feeling

on this subject is found in the vote recently cast by the Council of the National Economic League, whose members were asked to select from a list of subjects for public discussion, those which they considered of the most pressing importance. The Council consists of about eight hundred members, taken from every state in the Union, including presidents of universities, professors of political economy, judges, lawyers, bankers, merchants, manufacturers, and it represents all classes, interests, and opinions. The vote showed that these men placed "Direct Legislation," including primary nominations, the referendum and the recall, first, and "Inefficiency and Delay of the Courts in the Administration of Justice," second, in a list of eleven subjects, putting the latter far above the regulation of corporations, the centralization of power in the Federal Government, the conservation of national resources, taxation, economy, the relations of employers and workmen, and even the tariff. To my sorrow, I must confess that the Economic

## CONDITIONS OF THE PROBLEM

Club of my native city placed the inefficiency of the courts at the head of the list.

Indeed, to such a pitch has our profession fallen, that Mr. Roosevelt, after reflecting on its sins and shortcomings during his year in the wilds of Africa, had no sooner emerged from the jungle than he said:—"No people have permanently amounted to anything whose only public leaders were clerks, politicians, and *lawyers*." He found some virtue in the politician, adding:—"An honest, courageous, and farsighted politician is a good thing in any country . . . where the business man, the landowner, the engineer, the man of technical knowledge, men of a hundred different pursuits, represent the average type of leadership," but among all these possible leaders he found no room for the lawyer. Not "in his haste," but after long and solitary reflection, he places us lowest in the scale of citizenship, and condemns the lawyers of all time as well as those who incur his wrath to-day.

"No people have permanently amounted

to anything whose only leaders were clerks, politicians, and lawyers."

I am not inclined to accept this judgment. We might inquire what backward people in Africa or elsewhere has been kept from civilization by its lawyers. We might ask how the downfall of Palmyra or Babylon, the decay of Greece, Rome, the Ottoman Empire, or any other nation, can be traced to the predominance of the law. We might suggest that the Corpus Juris of Justinian is the most enduring monument of imperial Rome, and that Napoleon's most valuable legacy to the world is the Code which bears his name. We might even contend that our own country has amounted to something, although it has numbered among its leaders such lawyers as Hamilton, the Adamses, Jefferson, Marshall, Lincoln, Sumner, Cleveland, and Taft, and though of the twenty-eight Americans whose lives were thought worthy to be recorded in the series of biographies, entitled "American Statesmen," twenty were lawyers.

## CONDITIONS OF THE PROBLEM

We need not, however, stop there. We can go further, and point with pride to the great lawyers of every civilized country, and reply with absolute truth:

"No people have ever permanently amounted to anything among whose leaders great lawyers were *not* conspicuous and among whom respect for the law was not a controlling force."

Law is civilization, and the history of civilization is the record of the struggle between might and right — between force and law. Whatever may have been the sins of our profession, its members have ever been the champions and defenders of liberty, and the names of Cicero and Mazzini, of Grotius and Barneveldt, of Turgot, Danton, Thiers and Gambetta, Coke, Hampden, and Burke, of Grattan and O'Connell, not to mention American lawyers, recall only a few among such champions. The facts might not alter the opinion of our critic, but they completely answer his sneer.

We cannot, however, long retain our claim to

leadership, or even to the respect of the community unless we show ourselves able to do successfully the work which is especially ours, and to make the law an efficient instrument of justice. We cannot shut our ears to such words as I have quoted to you, and we must consider how much truth there is in these criticisms, and how the existing evils in the administration of the law can best be dealt with.

These questions are of peculiar interest to you who are just entering upon your professional lives, for ours is a very practical people, and if litigation becomes too tedious, too expensive, and too uncertain for ordinary men, clients will become extinct, and with them the support of the lawyer. We must make our methods suit their needs, and not waste their time and money in settling points of procedure or technical law, which may interest us but not them, remembering the remark of Lord Jeffrey, that "It is not by his own taste but by the taste of his fish that the angler is guided in his choice of bait." The problem is, therefore, severely practical, and upon you who bring to the work fresh strength and enthusiasm, who are not bound by the habits and the traditions which fetter the activity of your seniors, and who for a while at least may fairly expect the necessary leisure, upon you must fall the labor of reform. For those who will undertake and carry it through, the highest rewards of the profession are waiting. "*Sic itur ad astra.*"

I propose, in these lectures, to consider successively the evils which are pointed out by our critics, and to suggest, so far as I can, the possible remedies. The subject is old, and I may not tell you much that is new, but my aim is to make you think, and first I would let you appreciate the conditions of the problem, and its essential difficulties. Men frequently point to the advance which has been made in medicine and surgery, in physical science, and in mechanical invention during the last half century, and compare it with the lack of progress in the law, to the disadvantage of our profession. The comparison is most misleading. The whole community stands behind the scientific explorer or inventor, and rejoices in his success. Every man is glad when the remedy for diphtheria, or tuberculosis, or yellow fever is discovered, when Lister invents the antiseptic spray, when the aviator on his aeroplane crosses the Channel or the Alps, or when Edison brings the prima donna into our own parlors by the phonograph. Disease has no friends to insist that the surgeon shall continue to infect his patient, or the physician to reduce his strength by bleeding and drastic medicines. No strong interests are enlisted to support the physical ills which destroy us, and hence the progress of science is not only unopposed but aided by generous contributions even from "malefactors of great wealth." The way of the scientific reformer is smoothed before him.

Very different are the conditions which confront the man who would reform abuses in politics, in social life, or in the law. Upon

## CONDITIONS OF THE PROBLEM

every existing evil in either some one now fattens, and is sure to oppose a change. You cannot purify municipal politics without disturbing the many great and little "grafters," to use the modern phrase, who live by corruption. You cannot reduce the tariff without a battle against every man who finds his profit in the privileges given by the existing law. You cannot punish the boycott, or try to prevent the lawless excesses of the striker, without bringing down upon your head the anathemas of organized labor. You cannot assert the equal rights of the negro without encountering the bitter prejudice of the ignorant whites. Every form of legal or political injustice profits some one, and every step forward must be taken against his opposition.

So is it with reform in law. All the forces of tradition, of established habit, and in many cases of personal interest are united against reform, and the inertia of very busy men accustomed to existing methods and often too old to

## REFORM OF LEGAL PROCEDURE

learn new ones — of men, who are content to say, "Let well alone," without inquiring too closely whether it is "well" or not, — of men who are more prone to discuss than to act, is perhaps the strongest defence of old abuses, strongest, because it is honest. We must encounter also the differing opinions of sincere reformers, each proposing his own remedy, and only after hard conflict with both friends and enemies can we expect to advance. One can test the value of a discovery in medicine by its practical effect on selected cases. The result of a few experiments closes debate within a short time. The effect of a change in the law, or in legal procedure, cannot be tested as quickly or as easily, and hence must long remain a subject for discussion with consequent delay.

Now, fortunately, the leaders of the legal profession recognize the necessity of reform, and their feeling creates an atmosphere which is helpful. The conditions which await the reformers before me are as favorable as they are ever likely to be, and opportunity waits for him who has the strength and the courage to grasp it.

With this preliminary statement I will now proceed to the discussion of my subject, but before dealing with the abuses which do exist, let me first dispose of one which does not exist, but is made the ground of a serious charge against our profession.

In addressing the assembled alumni of Harvard, President Roosevelt said: "Many of the most influential and most highly remunerated members of the law in every centre of wealth make it their special task to work out bold and ingenious schemes by which their very wealthy clients, individual or corporate, can evade the laws which are made to regulate in the interest of the public the use of great wealth!" This is a very sweeping statement and invites analysis. It is founded on the very violent presumption that the legislature in passing a law has a clear and definite object in view, and that, to accomplish this object, it adopts clear and precise language which every citizen must understand. The fact of course is, that in most cases the law is drawn hastily to meet a real or supposed popular demand, that it is amended carelessly at the instance of members who are not thoroughly familiar with its provisions, that it means one thing to one legislator and another to another, that it is often passed with very slight debate, and that it not infrequently contains what is familiarly called "a joker," which has escaped the legislature's observation. The question which the lawyer and his client must decide is not what this or that legislator thought he was doing, nor even what the President believed to be the purpose of the law which he approved, but what the legislature as a whole meant, and this meaning can only be ascertained from the language of the law itself.

The Supreme Court of the United States, in a series of cases, has labored long and carefully to discover what the Sherman anti-trust law

## CONDITIONS OF THE PROBLEM

means, and the justices have rarely agreed. They have now for many months been considering how it shall be applied to the greatest, and, to the public, the most obnoxious trust in the country. The Interstate Commerce Act has been the subject of long and painful study in the courts. All our judges have like difficulties with legislative enactments. It is not strange, therefore, that the meaning of a new law should not at once be apparent to the ordinary citizen, and that when the law interferes with an existing practice or course of dealing, the question in many cases should arise, how far this interference goes. That question is submitted to counsel, and it is a very practical question. The lawyer answers it as best he may, saying that the law forbids this and permits that, and in giving his answer to such a question he decides what the words of the statute mean — what the legislature has in fact done. This conclusion may or may not agree with what individual legislators or the President meant to do, but an

## REFORM OF LEGAL PROCEDURE

intention to pass a law is one thing, and the law itself is another. When our critic says that eminent lawyers are "working out bold and ingenious schemes by which their . . . clients . . . can evade the laws" they are really telling their clients what the law permits, and how to make their practice comply with its requirements.

This is not evading but obeying the law, and because even the most exalted citizen finds that the law does not accomplish what *he* thinks proper, he has no right to criticize those who act under the law which *the legislature* thought proper, for they obey the law as it is, and not the opinion of an orator as to what the law ought to be. A counsel would be indeed at sea who should seek to advise his clients not to do what a president or governor thinks they ought not to do, and would have greater difficulty in discovering either officer's desire from his utterances on the platform and in reconciling his varying statements, than he has in construing the blind language of the statute itself. Fortu-

## CONDITIONS OF THE PROBLEM

nately for us all, the law is not made by a stump speech or even by a President's message. Our rulers are not despots who govern by edict.

That there are cases where lawyers help their clients to do things which are improper and unlawful is unhappily true, as there are manufacturers who produce fraudulent goods, doctors who perform illegal operations, and magistrates who disregard the constitution and the laws which they have sworn to obey and execute; but the sweeping statement which I have quoted is one of many like attacks on Bar and Bench alike, which are entirely unjustified or grossly exaggerated, and which do great injury by weakening that respect for the law and its administration which Mr. Roosevelt in a different mood has rightly called "the corner-stone of this republic."

Let us now proceed to consider the real evils which beset the administration of justice, and first among them is "the law's delay"—an evil which has been the cause of bitter complaint ever since legal tribunals came into being. The barons of England made their king promise in these words:

"*Nulli negabimus, nulli vendemus, nulli differemus rectum vel justitiam,*" putting the delay on the same plane with the denial or sale of justice. The author of Hamlet, whether a Lord Chancellor or a humble poet, places it among the intolerable burdens of life which a man might well escape by suicide. It has been a favorite theme with novelists, and always a constant topic in the conversation of clients and their friends, never more so than now.

But in considering how to remedy it, we must first remember that some delay is necessary and beneficial. As I have said in another place, —

The courts are called upon to decide disputed questions of fact and law on which the parties find it impossible to agree, and in order to decide, there must be patient investigation. The careful examination of any subject takes time. The chemist in his laboratory, the historian in his

## CONDITIONS OF THE PROBLEM

library, the astronomer in his observatory, spends a great deal of time in reaching the conclusions which he announces to the world in a few words; but the time which he spends is his own, and the world does not know how many hours of labor have gone into researches of which the fruits only are laid before it. The difference between investigations which are made by courts and those which are made by students and inventors, is that the latter do their work in private and use their own time, while the courts do their work in public and use time for which the public pays. In order to investigate properly, they call upon some citizens to act as jurors and draw others into court as witnesses. The whole community sees how long the investigation takes, and what it costs, and therefore the law's delay is more in the public eye than the delay of private investigators.

At the same time, this delay is what the public wants. It demands investigation. Nothing is more vexing, more proverbially un-

## REFORM OF LEGAL PROCEDURE

sound, than a "snap judgment." The decisions of the courts not only decide the rights of the immediate litigants in the case at bar, but they also lay down precedents which establish the rights of all. A man wants his architect, when he is building a house, to make the plans carefully; he wants his doctor, when he examines his symptoms, to make sure that the examination is thorough; and he wants the courts, when they decide the rules by which men are to be guided in their daily life, to be thorough, also. The public wants no capricious, hasty judgments, but that justice which is done by careful, patient investigation, and such an investigation takes time, which is another word for delay.

Not only that, but a certain amount of delay is essential in order that the case may be fairly tried. The plaintiff can bring his suit whenever he sees fit. The defendant has no control over that. A claim may be entirely unfounded, but it may take a great while to collect the witnesses

## CONDITIONS OF THE PROBLEM

from various parts of the world to prove the truth. It takes time to examine books; it takes time to look through letters; it takes time for the defendant to marshal the evidence which is necessary to show that the plaintiff's claim is groundless. When a man comes forward, as did the Tichborne claimant in England, asserting his right to an ancient title and a large estate, and having carefully prepared his claim in advance, the defendant must have time to prepare his defense — to follow the pretender's career from its beginning, and to prove that he is really only a butcher. The trial of that case took more than six months. The preparation could not be made without long and patient investigation. This is one reason why delay is incident to the law.

Nor is delay entirely undesirable. Men in hot blood rush to their lawyers with some complaint. They want something done at once, and a writ is issued. Then they ask what comes next, and are told that in perhaps thirty days the

## REFORM OF LEGAL PROCEDURE

case will be entered, that the other side has then thirty days in which to file an answer; and that very likely the case may be reached in a year or more. They have time to cool; and many a suit which would be tried, if it could be tried in a week, with great heat and bad feeling between the combatants, and with much expense to the public as well as to the parties, is settled before it is reached, because the parties have had time to think it over and to reach an amicable adjustment. Such delay is extremely useful.

In this connection a few figures may be of interest. In England, in 1905, there were brought 1,213,000 suits, and of those, 349,200 were defaulted; 440,300 were settled; less than one-third were tried. The proportion is about the same here, and these amicable and economical adjustments are secured by delay.

So much can be said in favor of reasonable and desirable delay, but there is much that is entirely preventable and which is neither reasonable nor desirable. It is this which does

## CONDITIONS OF THE PROBLEM

cruel wrong to clients, and justly brings reproach on the law. What are its causes?

This delay may occur in bringing a case to trial, in the trial itself, or in the proceedings after the trial. Its causes are to be found partly in the lawyers, partly in the courts, and partly in the rules which regulate procedure and appeal, and before proceeding to consider how these causes are to be removed, there are certain fundamental propositions which must be borne in mind, and which I will endeavor to state briefly.

A lawsuit is the means which the government provides for settling peaceably a question upon which the parties cannot agree. It is for the interest of the parties and of the community that this question should be settled promptly and the dispute ended, for it is true, in small matters as well as in great, that unsettled questions have no respect for the repose of nations or men. The cost of the machinery which the state provides for the purpose, the courthouses, the

## REFORM OF LEGAL PROCEDURE

judges, the jurors, the officers, is borne by the public, and the public is entitled to be saved all unnecessary expense. The lawyers who conduct the proceedings are officers of the Court, intended and expected to aid it in reaching a just conclusion, and therefore given great powers and privileges. The parties are entitled to a fair trial of the facts either by jury or Court, to a careful consideration of all questions of law involved by a competent tribunal, and to nothing more. In a large majority of cases, three months and often less is ample time to give for preparation or for settlement. Delay beyond that dulls the memory of witnesses, it prevents the plaintiff in a suit for personal injury from getting well, since he must be sick when the case is tried, it keeps a creditor out of money which perhaps he sorely needs, it diverts the thoughts of the parties from their ordinary work, and it increases expense. Yet, in all our large cities, the delay is far greater, since often two or more years will elapse before a case is reached for trial.

CONDITIONS OF THE PROBLEM

What are the causes of this delay? For how much of it are the members of the Bar responsible? To answer this question, we must have some standard by which to measure the responsibilities of counsel. Lord Brougham, in the excitement of his argument for Queen Caroline, some ninety years ago said:

"An advocate, by the sacred duty which he owes his client, knows, in the discharge of that office, but one person in the world — that client and none other. To save that client by all means and expedients, to protect that client at all hazards and costs to all others, and among others to himself, is the highest and most unquestioned of his duties; and he must not regard the alarm, the suffering, the torment, the destruction, which he may bring upon any other. Nay, separating the duties of the patriot from those of an advocate, he must go on, reckless of consequences, even if his fate should unhappily be to involve his country in confusion for his client's protection."

REFORM OF LEGAL PROCEDURE

Whether in a soberer moment Lord Brougham would have defended this position may well be doubted, but whatever his view, it is certain that no such pernicious doctrine can be supported for a moment. Brougham makes no distinction between the client who is guilty and one who is innocent, between justice and injustice, between right and wrong. In every state, in one form or another, the lawyer is required by the attorney's oath to repudiate any such obligation to his client. I quote the Massachusetts form as it is most familiar to me. Its language is:

"I solemnly swear that I will do no falsehood, nor consent to the doing of any in court; I will not wittingly or willingly promote or sue any false, groundless, or unlawful suit, nor give aid or consent to the same; I will delay no man for lucre or malice; but I will conduct myself in the office of an attorney within the courts according to the best of my knowledge and discretion and with all good fidelity as well to the courts as my clients."

## CONDITIONS OF THE PROBLEM

This states the lawyer's duty, as it is. Let me quote also the Code of Ethics, lately adopted by the Bar of San Francisco, inspired, doubtless, by the recent lamentable experiences of justice in that city. Though in terms it refers only to criminal cases, its principle applies as well in all cases.

"A lawyer, who invents or manufactures defenses for prisoners, or who procures their acquittal by the practice of any manner of deceit, cajolery, wilful distortion, or misrepresentation of facts, or any other means not within the spirit as well as the letter of the law, is to be reckoned as an enemy to society more dangerous than the criminal himself; while successes at the bar won by such methods can never be the basis of desirable professional reputations, but, on the contrary, are badges of infamy."

Let us now apply this standard to the proceedings before trial, the bringing of a suit, the pleadings in defence, and the speeding of the cause. The attorney's oath imposes on him who takes it, not only an obligation to his client, but to his client's adversary. He must pursue no man unjustly, nor must he delay any man for lucre. In brief, he must bring no suit unless in his judgment it can be maintained, and he must interpose no defence to a just suit because his client wishes to delay or embarrass his opponent. One great cause of delay in the law is the congestion of the dockets, and no one can doubt that this congestion would be much reduced if all the suits which ought never to have been brought, and those which ought not to be defended, were eliminated. Some years ago, in Massachusetts, when money was worth as much as the interest allowed by the law, it was the regular practice for men who were sued on their notes or other undisputed claims to file an answer denying the plaintiff's allegations, and then agree that when the case was reached the defendant should be defaulted. The condition of the docket was such that, in this way, the debtor secured a year or more of delay at very slight expense.

## CONDITIONS OF THE PROBLEM

The lawyer who was paid to file such an answer for the debtor and to make such an agreement was clearly delaying the creditor for lucre, and abusing his power as an attorney.

Far too often do we hear of men saying to others who press their just claims, "If you won't take my offer I'll hire a lawyer and make you pay for everything you get." Every one knows that the debtor can carry out his threat, and will do so if he is rich enough to afford it or malicious enough to wish it. Is it surprising that the community believes that a lawyer can be hired to do anything, and can it truly be said that this belief is unfounded? So long as there are bad clients there will be bad lawyers, and we cannot expect that either will wholly disappear, but the profession suffers in public estimation from the acts of its black sheep, and every honorable lawyer should struggle against their practices, and be sure that his example is good.

The delay which results from the bringing of groundless suits and the making of false defences

## REFORM OF LEGAL PROCEDURE

is due to low professional standards among members of the Bar, and is to be cured by creating a public opinion which will not tolerate such practices. But it can also be diminished by legislation. The practice of obstructing the collection of debts in Massachusetts (to which I have alluded) was ended by a statute which enabled the creditor, by filing an affidavit that the debtor had no defence, to make the latter state his defence in a counter affidavit. If he did not he was defaulted, and if he did the statute authorized the Court thereupon to direct an immediate trial of the case. The possible delay was in this way so much reduced that the Courts ceased to be a bulwark for unjust debtors.

A further step in the same direction might be taken if the Courts were given discretion to fix the amount of costs to be paid by the losing party. In theory the costs are intended to cover the expense to which the prevailing party is put by his opponent. In practice they are

## CONDITIONS OF THE PROBLEM

but a drop in the bucket. The cost of printing a voluminous record is reimbursed — some fraction of what it costs to print a brief is returned, but the charges of counsel, the fees of expert witnesses, and other expenses must be paid by the victor out of his own pocket, and these may well make victory more costly than surrender without a contest. Under existing law it costs little to start a groundless suit, in order to frighten an adversary, or take a speculative chance of getting a settlement. It costs very little by various methods to delay a suitor until he is wearied or worried into a compromise. If he who would thus abuse the law knew that he might be compelled to pay every dollar of expense to which he put his opponent, he would hesitate.

There are many cases in which the question presented, whether of fact or law, is very doubtful, and in these it might be unjust to punish the losing party by imposing very heavy costs; but if the Court were given proper discretion it would easily discriminate, and only impose the heavy costs where justice required it. In many cases, justice is not done now, because the suitor who seeks only what is justly due him is mulcted severely by the cost of recovering what is his own, and he is put to this cost by the evil practices of his opponent. Why should not the latter pay the damages which his wrongful act has inflicted on another, just as he must pay the damages inflicted by any other tortious act? A wrong committed in obstructing justice is no more venial than any other wrong.

It would be well also if the Court more freely used its power to punish the lawyer who has lent his talents to injustice, and has harried or delayed a man wrongly for lucre. This could readily be done by making him personally pay the expenses which the opposing party has been compelled to incur unjustly. The English Courts have adopted a rule which permits this, and which reads as follows:

"If in any case it shall appear to the Court

## CONDITIONS OF THE PROBLEM

or a judge that costs have been improperly or without any reasonable cause incurred, or that by reason of any undue delay in proceeding under any judgment or order or of any misconduct or default of the solicitor, any costs properly incurred have nevertheless proved fruitless to the person incurring the same, the Court or judge may call on the solicitor of the person by whom such costs have been so incurred to shew cause why such should not be disallowed as between the solicitor and his client, and also (if the circumstances of the case shall require) why the solicitor should not repay to his client any costs which the client may have been ordered to pay to any other person, and thereupon may make such order as the justice of the case any require."

This rule was applied in *Harbin* v. *Masterman*, L. R. 1st Chan. Div., where the Court made the solicitor himself pay the client because his appeal was frivolous, and, as the judges called it, "a blackmailing appeal for the purpose of compelling his opponents to forego their costs."

REFORM OF LEGAL PROCEDURE

If the Court had this power, and stood ready to use it, and if the costs that could be recovered were substantial and not nominal, a very wholesome check would be imposed upon unjust litigation, and the lawyer would be led to feel his personal responsibility much more keenly. There is little danger that judges would abuse this power, and what reasonable objection exists to giving it? We may well borrow this expedient from England. This is one of many things in which we should give the Courts more power.

But you may say that I am setting too high a standard for the lawyer, a standard higher than is accepted generally by the Bar. Very likely; but I am trying to show you why the Bar is losing ground with the public, and it may well be that among the causes is the fact that the standards of practice are too low. Be not afraid, however, of too high a standard. The danger is not here. Strive as we may, it is impossible, in the fierce struggles of life, in the controversies of the Bar, in the heat of the jury

## CONDITIONS OF THE PROBLEM

trial, not to fall below the ideals of our cooler moments. Be they as high as we can make them, there is no danger that our practice will reach too high a level. What is true of every man in every walk of life is especially true of the lawyer, whose temptations are peculiarly great.

It is doubtless hard for the young lawyer, who must have work or starve, to say that he will not bring a suit or interpose a defence which his client will pay him for doing. When refusal means not only loss of money which is sorely needed, but perhaps exposes him to the contempt of active men who think a lawyer should at least be pliable, it is very hard to refuse. Yet nothing will pay the lawyer so well as such a refusal. There is no asset so precious to him as character. "Remember, young man," said Charles Sumner, "that character is everything." There is always a demand for honesty. No matter how unscrupulous a man may be in his business, no matter how much he may value the services of a rascal in furthering his own rascality during his life, — when he comes to die he wishes to leave his property in honest hands for the sake of his wife and his children. The majority of men — I think the large majority — are honest and love honest men. The lawyer who stands in a community for incorruptible honesty acquires an influence which is invaluable. When it is known that his presence in Court means that he thinks his client right, that mere presence has great weight with jury or with Court. The services of such a man are sought by all, and the client is fortunate who secures them. Positions of honor and trust seek him, and if his success is slow, it is sure and lasting. To such men, only, come the highest rewards of our profession.

Do you want an example of this truth? Let me give you Abraham Lincoln, of whom his biographer says:

"He was preëminently the honest lawyer, the counsel fitted to serve the litigant who was justly entitled to win. . . . He generally refused

## CONDITIONS OF THE PROBLEM

to take cases unless he could see that, as a matter of genuine right, he ought to win. People who consulted him were at times bluntly advised to withdraw from an unjust or a hard-hearted contention, or were bidden to seek other counsel. He could even go the length of leaving a case, while actually conducting it, if he became satisfied of unfairness on the part of his client. . . . Those who are not members of this ingenious profession, contemning the fine logic which they fail to overcome, stubbornly insist upon admiring the lawyer who refuses to subordinate right to law."

It was thus that he acquired the title of "honest old Abe," and under that title he won the Presidency of the United States. By that sign he conquered. We cannot all be Presidents, but the course which gave him that great office may win for each of us the smaller measure of success to which we are respectively entitled. Honesty may not win, but dishonesty must in the long run lose. "Corruption wins not more than honesty," says Shakespeare, and it should be added, that what corruption wins is not worth winning. Full many an old man, both in and out of our profession, would give all the wealth that he has gained in exchange for the respect of his fellows and the confidence of the community, which he forfeited in gaining it.

But there is another sin of the Bar, deep-rooted in our imperfect human nature, which is responsible for much unnecessary delay. It has been said by many, and every old lawyer recognizes its truth, that no man however well prepared, however confident of success, however sincerely he may insist upon a trial, ever fails to feel a sense of relief, when, against his most earnest efforts, the trial is postponed. It is the only professional defeat which a lawyer accepts with equanimity, nay even with gratitude. You, gentlemen, as students have learned to know and dread an examination. A trial is a severe competitive examination,

## CONDITIONS OF THE PROBLEM

not lasting for a few hours, with results that attract no public attention, but lasting sometimes for weeks, under the public eye, involving to the counsel engaged their reputations for skill and ability, and calling upon every resource that the combatants can command. It means long days under the severest strain upon eye, ear, nerves, and temper; it means long evenings of labor on evidence or law; it means sleepless nights; it means being absolutely possessed by one subject to the exclusion of every other thought while the trial lasts, and it may well mean at the end a defeat which is felt to be unmerited, followed by a period of exhaustion, and idle criticism of self, opponents, jurors, witnesses, and judges. This is an ordeal which a man dislikes to face, and experience does not make it more attractive. The young lawyer rushes into court, confident in the justice of his cause. His older brother is dragged in, knowing how uncertain the result of a trial always must be, never so much alarmed as when

## REFORM OF LEGAL PROCEDURE

his case seems absolutely sure and he can see no ground on which his opponent can win. He realizes, with Mr. Justice Curtis, that "Every new witness is a new peril," and he knows all the chances of battle. Is it surprising that postponements are easily arranged, and that hard cases are long delayed? When the opposing counsel asks for delay, because his convenience or his other engagements or his need of rest make it desirable, it is very hard to refuse. Professional courtesy is appealed to, and, as he who draws the sword shall perish by the sword, so he who refuses his associates such favors may find his own requests denied at some moment of supreme exigency. Thus we get into the habit of readily consenting to delay for the convenience of counsel at the expense of clients.

This is a very serious evil. Some time ago, a man sought me, and said that certain former partners owed him $150,000, but refused to pay it, and a suit for the settlement of his accounts had been pending for six years. On the opposite

## CONDITIONS OF THE PROBLEM

sides were engaged two leading seniors and two very able and very busy juniors. When one senior was at home, he said, the other was away; when one junior was at liberty the other was engaged in a trial, and the result was that appointment after appointment for hearing was made and broken, and perhaps two or three days out of a year were actually given to the trial of the case before a Master. Meanwhile, he was growing older, crippled by not having his money, and wholly unable to see a way out of his difficulties. He asked me what he was to do, and whether I would take his case. I told him that I could not do so. He had as able counsel as there were at the Bar, and I could not displace them. They were thoroughly familiar with his case, and I could add nothing, while it would cost much to give me the knowledge of his case which they had. I could only advise him that he must make himself peculiarly disagreeable to his counsel until they tried the case. This is merely an illustration which may enable you to tell why the public complains of the law's delay.

Conscious as I am of my own weakness, I can suggest no remedy for this evil other than the cultivation of a higher standard among the members of the Bar. Laziness, a certain cowardice, and the conflicting demands of numerous clients, are the causes of this delay. In such matters, the Bar should adopt the rule of Lord Brougham, and if the interests of the client demand a speedy trial, no convenience of his own or his opponent's, no laziness, no cowardice, should relax his efforts to speed the cause. Courtesy to his professional brother may well be cruelty to the man whose interests are confided to his care, and should not prevail. The remedy for delays thus caused is a keener professional conscience.

A most prolific cause of delay in reaching a trial is found in the conflicting engagements of counsel. As an eminent lawyer once remarked, as the result of long experience: "I have never found any court that could compel me to be in two places at the same time." The clients of a busy lawyer perhaps cannot complain if they have to take their turns. They employ him with their eyes open, for the same reason that others want him. His opponents, however, have no choice, and a client may often secure long delay, simply by employing a counsel who is much engaged. It is very difficult, in practice, to force such a lawyer into the trial of any case that he does not wish to try, for he can always choose some other engagement, at least for a considerable time. To quote the words of a commission appointed in Massachusetts last year to consider and report on delay in civil actions: "A busy lawyer may by reason of his numerous engagements readily render impossible the trial of a particular case which his adversary wishes to try." In England, the courts do not recognize an engagement in one court as a reason for not trying a case when it is reached in another court. The result is that clients suffer in another way, for as no lawyer, when he is retained, can absolutely foresee what his engagements may be when the case is called for trial, clients engage two barristers, senior and junior, that the junior may try the case if the senior happens to be engaged. Thus they may pay for the services of a lawyer, and not get what they pay for, while the expense is increased by the necessity of employing two counsel. I think, however, that this rule, if persisted in, will work well in the end. Clients will not long pay for what they do not get, and either counsel and court will so arrange assignments as to avoid conflicts, or lawyers will not assume obligations which they cannot fulfil and practice will be distributed more widely. "Where there's a will, there's a way." There are many cases which require only ordinary professional skill, and counsel with large practice will employ such assistance as is necessary to deal with it promptly, instructing their juniors in many cases, and reserving themselves for such as call for greater ability or experience. Were the Courts less

## CONDITIONS OF THE PROBLEM

ready to accept the excuse of another engagement, the Bar would be driven to find a remedy, and it might be well to try the English rule.

## II

### *THE REDUCTION OF LITIGATION BY LEGISLATION*

AFTER giving full effect to all the causes which I have thus far suggested, there remains the congestion of the docket, the fact that cases are brought far faster than they can be tried, and the inevitable accumulation of work. What is the remedy for this?

The first remedy which I would suggest is the removal, by proper legislation, of what causes litigation. Years ago, the courts were largely occupied with disputes about the boundaries of, or title to real estate. We find the traces of this litigation in the novels and light literature of the day, as when Dandie Dinmont was anxious to have a lawsuit with his neighbor over a few feet of land, enough, as he said, "to feed a hog or

## REDUCTION OF LITIGATION

aiblins twa in a good year." The registration of deeds, with good surveying and careful examination of titles, has ended this so completely that litigation of this kind has almost disappeared. Some forty years ago when I entered perhaps the busiest office in Boston, there was no real action on its large docket, nor in many years of active practice since have I ever been asked to bring or defend such an action.

Not so many years ago, suits against insurance companies were very common. Now, owing in part to more carefully drawn policies, and in part to the fact that companies which contest claims lose business, insurance cases are rare. Such disputes are settled by agreement or arbitration.

To-day, actions to recover damages for personal injuries choke the courts. They have increased, and are increasing, at a rate entirely out of proportion to the increase of population. In Boston, such suits against street railways consume three quarters at least of the time given to jury trials, while much of the remainder is occupied with suits against other carriers, and suits by employees against their employers. This litigation, from every point of view, is wasteful and injurious to the community. A person injured by an accident and obliged to sue for damages, knows that on the extent and permanence of the injury depends the amount of the verdict, and hence until the case is ended is reasonably certain to languish. During the whole interval between suit and trial, he is preparing his case, watching his symptoms, registering his uncomfortable feelings, and, in short, exactly reversing the process by which professors of Christian Science cure their patients. He cannot afford to feel well, much less to recover entirely, and good doctors agree that in these circumstances imagination increases the victim's ills, and retards or even prevents his recovery. A man who wishes to get well will often do so, when one who does not may become a permanent invalid. If the trial results in defeat, this evil consequence remains, unmitigated by damages and very likely increased by the charges of the lawsuit. If, on the other hand, he recovers damages, the share which he gets seems affluence and is often spent recklessly, while the period between the accident and the end of the money recovered destroys the habits of work and thrift, and the real injury is multiplied many fold by the whole process. I remember once hearing the question raised in a large party of leading lawyers familiar with such cases, whether the recovery of damages in an accident suit benefited the successful suitor, and with one accord they agreed that they had never known a case where the damages had really done anything but harm.

The prosecution of such suits becomes a business by itself, and in every large community there are lawyers with offices equipped to gather and press such claims. They have runners who visit the injured, doctors who send them cases and testify for the claimants, experts upon whom

## REFORM OF LEGAL PROCEDURE

they rely, and if we believe all that is said by their enemies, they have also false witnesses, who testify at safe intervals to having seen the essential facts, and secret methods of reaching jurors. These men prevent amicable adjustments, inflate the injured person's ideas of damages, and regard their clients too often only as a means of extorting money from some other person for their own benefit. Their business is frequently legalized piracy, and they plunder both clients and opponents.

The medical profession is much exercised over the manner in which medical questions are tried, and mortified by the credence given to charlatans who pose as doctors. More and more the best physicians hesitate to testify as witnesses, because they cannot afford to waste their time in court waiting to be called, because they resent the cross-examination to which they are exposed, and because they dislike to become known as professional experts, recalling perhaps the dictum of the English judge who said there are three classes of false witnesses: "Liars, damned liars and experts." The system tends steadily to drive the competent physician out of court, and to bring the incompetent in. The circumstances and results of the accident often excite warm sympathy, and the jurymen are urged to compensate one who needs money at the expense of a rich employer without regard to the merits of the case, and so to disregard their oaths.

In a word, the system degrades the members of two great professions, the legal and the medical; it chokes the courts with lawsuits of which one half are without merit, it demoralizes the juries, and it injures even the successful litigant. Moreover, it chills the natural sympathy which might be felt for the injured person, and breeds hostility between employer and employee, since the employer is afraid to help, lest his doing so be regarded as an admission of liability, while the absence of such help is naturally treated by the victim as evidence of indifference to his sufferings.

Finally, the system entails an enormous expense

on the community. The cost of a single jury session in Boston is estimated by the Commission of which I spoke at $30,000 a year in the salaries of judge, clerk, court officers, and jurors' fees, alone. If we add to this the incidentals, fire, light, cleaning, repairs, and the interest on the large sum spent in providing and maintaining the courtroom, the total is far greater. There were seven such sessions in the Superior Court of Boston alone, in the year 1909, and more than three quarters of their time was spent in trying 615 tort cases, of which 210 resulted in verdicts for the plaintiff and 58 were settled during the trial. There were 30 disagreements, and in the other 317 cases the verdicts were for the defendant, so that judged by results more than half the claims which were brought to trial were unfounded. The recoveries in the other cases were generally small, and although the figures were not tabulated, I think it safe to say that the total amount recovered by the successful plaintiffs was less than the sum paid by the

## REDUCTION OF LITIGATION

taxpayers of Boston for trying their cases. Add to this the amount paid lawyers, witnesses, experts, stenographers, and for various incidentals by the parties on both sides, and the amount spent to accomplish this result is enormously increased.

Nor does the account end here. The danger of loss from accident claims has led almost all large employers of labor and most prudent citizens to insure themselves against liability for such claims, and the total amount paid in premiums is very large. Some idea of its amount may be derived from the report made last March to the Legislature of New York, by a special Commission. This shows that nine companies in three years received in premiums more than twenty-three and a half million dollars, of which they paid for claims covered by the insurance only about eight and a half millions, or 36.34 per cent. of what they received. The rest went to men employed as counsel or otherwise to defeat the claims or solicit new business, to the cost of administration and to profit. The community therefore contributes every year an enormous fund, partly in taxes and partly in premiums to insurance companies, and of this only a very small percentage goes to the parties injured.

These expenses when paid out of the taxes are a direct burden on the community. When paid by the employer they are an expense of his business, and a goodly portion of them certainly finds its way into the price charged for his goods. In this way the community again pays. The disabled workman who has recovered no compensation, and the disabled workman who has spent his money recklessly, with his family, often become charges upon public or private benevolence, and thus again the loss falls upon the public, so that a considerable fraction of what we call "the high cost of living" can certainly be traced to the waste and expense caused by accidents to workmen.

On the other hand, it is right—nay, more, it is necessary that men who are injured, certainly

## REDUCTION OF LITIGATION

those who are permanently disabled by accidents, should be supported. We cannot leave them to perish. The line between the accidents for which the employer is liable, and those of which the employee must bear the consequences, is not easy to draw. The questions of fact are close, the evidence is conflicting. The plaintiff's path is beset "with pitfall and with gin." The trial judge and the appellate court often differ as to the law, the jury often differs, and while disagreements are comparatively rare, the difference finds expression in reduced damages. When the courts first held that a judge might direct a verdict for the defendant, if there was no evidence of neglect by the defendant, or was clear evidence of contributory neglect by the plaintiff, but in doubtful cases must submit the case to the jury, counsel in arguing asked the Court: "Do your Honors mean to hold that the easy cases are for the Court and the hard cases for the jury?" This in a nutshell states the rule.

In many cases there is no negligence on either

side, but a pure accident which no one could reasonably anticipate, as when a workman going to a pile of scrap iron, which he was expected to use as needed, in pulling out a piece released a steel spring, which, striking him in the eye, put it out and so disabled a fine young man for life. Some fellow-workman had thrown the spring on the pile.

In the great iron mills, in the mines, in great manufacturing establishments of every kind, a more or less steady percentage of the workmen are killed or disabled, and to put the matter on the lowest plane, this loss should be treated as an expense of the business, to be paid and reckoned in the price of goods as much as the destruction of machinery, the wearing out of tools, the spoiling of materials, or any other thing which may be covered by the wear and tear of plant.

When to the mere material considerations we add the moral obligation to help our fellow men in distress, the argument is overwhelming.

REDUCTION OF LITIGATION

The question is, how to save the present enormous waste, and how to secure the injured employee proper compensation without injustice to his employer. If we can devise a scheme by which the money which the employer now pays for insurance or for expenses and losses, the money which the injured man pays for counsel and the other costs of litigation, and the money which the community pays for the judges, jurors, and others whose time is spent in dealing with these questions, or for supporting helpless workmen and their families, can be used directly to provide for the victims of accident, the gain to the general body of citizens in every way will be enormous, and the saving in money alone may well be large. To this problem the people of every country where industrial development is considerable are devoting much time and thought, and this country among others is studying it. The solution is not yet found, and you, gentlemen, will be confronted with it when you begin practice. In your time it will be settled, probably, and some of you may win fame by contributing to this settlement. Upon you all will rest the duty of trying.

With us the problem is complicated by two considerations.

*First*, the power of our legislatures is fettered by constitutional restrictions, and

*Second*, no state can afford to lay upon its citizens who employ labor a greater burden than is imposed by other states upon their citizens, lest capital seek the state where the burden is lightest.

To a certain extent, the last consideration applies between the competing nations of Europe. They seek the same markets, and Germany cannot afford to make the manufacturing cost of goods greater than it is in England or France. But it is not so easy to move a manufacturing plant and its operatives from Germany to France, as it is to move it from Massachusetts to Maine or New Hampshire.

On the other hand, a good law adopted in

one state spreads rapidly over the country; the demand of the laborer for the best law is a force which influences every legislature, and while the necessity of uniform legislation may delay, it cannot prevent a proper solution of the problem. It is so obviously demanded by every consideration, moral and economic, that the strong common sense of the American people will find it.

Within the limits of these lectures it is impossible to discuss the various systems adopted or proposed in different countries or states, but some general suggestions may be made. No constitution prevents men from contracting freely with each other, and we may first consider what may be done by contracts of workmen with each other, of employers with each other, and of workmen with employers.

We find, in the first place, a large body of insurers who stand ready for a certain premium to insure any man against accident whether caused by his carelessness or not. Could an adequate fund be raised to pay the premiums necessary to insure every workman against accident, so that he would be sure to receive a fixed sum in case of injury, the same provision would be made for him and his family that the ordinarily prudent man makes when he insures his life or takes out a policy against accidents, and the workman might well agree to accept this certainty in place of the uncertainty, anxiety, expense, and other evils which attend his present right to sue his employer. Where is this premium fund to be found?

In the first place, a certain contribution might be made out of his wages by the workman himself. It is not too much to ask that every man make some provision against the chances of life, or in the common phrase, "lay up something for a rainy day." To do this is to encourage habits of thrift which are in themselves desirable, to say nothing of other advantages. There are now mutual benefit associations, burial societies, and like organizations, to which workmen contribute, the general plan being that each member pays a small more or less regular assessment thus creating a fund out of which salaries and expenses are provided, and when members die or are disabled, certain sums are paid to themselves or their families. As a rule, the assessment which is sufficient when members are numerous and young, is likely to be too small as the original members grow old and deaths are more frequent, and these associations perish because their mathematical calculations are wrong, in which event the surviving members lose. This method of insurance is unwise and uneconomical, and the money spent in it can be spent more wisely. Under a proper system such contributions as these might be made the nucleus of the premium fund.

Among enlightened employers, the system of profit-sharing as a means of giving the workman adequate wages is becoming more common, and from the money which the workmen would

## REFORM OF LEGAL PROCEDURE

receive under this system, something might well be taken to increase it. The money which the employer now pays for liability insurance and for the expenses connected with claims by workmen might be added to the fund without in the least enhancing his present expense.

Moreover, by association between employers in different lines of business, mutual insurance companies could be formed which would lessen the individual risk and the total expense. For insurance against fire, such mutual insurance companies have existed for years, and have accomplished the most excellent results. They have compelled parties who sought insurance to take proper precautions against fire, and having studied the causes of fire and the methods of prevention, they have been able to point out in each case what must be done. This system has naturally reduced the loss by fire, and as a result the cost of insurance has become almost nominal to the parties insured in these companies. As no manufacturer can afford to pay more for insurance or any other expense of his business than his competitors, all desire to become members of the mutual companies, and to do this all must comply with the requirements of these companies.

Were the same system adopted for insurance against accident, there would be a thorough inspection of the premises occupied by an applicant for insurance, and he would be required by protecting his machines and in other ways to take proper precautions. The causes of accident would be studied carefully, and, as in the case of fire, new precautions would be devised from time to time. Regular inspection by the agents of the insurance companies would insure the observance of proper rules, and as a result the number of accidents would be reduced and consequently the cost of insurance. The employer would find it wise to do what the insurance company required in order to reduce the cost of insurance, and the standard of care which such an insurance company should fix, would become the standard by which in case of accident every employer would be judged.

Not only would the necessary contribution to the premium fund be reduced by diminishing the chances of accident, but in other ways. The insurer against liability for accident now includes in his premium not only what is needed to pay losses, but also what is needed to pay the expenses of resisting claims, and his own profit. These two items with the expenses of management take some 65 per cent. of the premium. If, however, the insurer agreed to pay a definite sum in case of accident whether caused by negligence or not, the expense of resisting claims would be largely eliminated, and as the profit of the mutual company is used to reduce premiums, this also would disappear. Hence the premium required would on these accounts be reduced, while the absolute liability might make the losses greater and so increase the premium, unless, as has happened with fires, the precautions against accident which the mutual com-

## REDUCTION OF LITIGATION

pany required should reduce the number of accidents enough or more than enough to offset the loss from greater liability. It should be borne in mind that the employer's premium is now fixed by considerations drawn from experience with many unconnected employers, and that having paid it he is somewhat indifferent to accidents. If every accident increased the expense of insurance, all employers would be more careful. It is probable that the employer's contribution to our premium fund might be less than he now pays for insurance against liability.

We have, so far, as contributors to the fund, the employee and the employer. Might not the State also contribute? If the argument is sound, the State will save much in the expense of courts and much in the support of the poor. It will gain also something through the removal of one cause which produces friction and bad relations between employer and employed. Can it properly be asked out of these savings to pay anything towards the premium fund? Suppose the general scheme of mutual insurance is extended so as to cover disability caused by age as well as by accident, so that in a way it provides an old age pension. This is delicate ground, but it must be remembered that every poorhouse contains its old age pensioners. Out-door relief is often only an old age pension. The helpless are supported, if by no one else, by the public. Could not this relief be given through public contribution to a system which would provide for such pensioners? The State now takes money from the taxpayer, and gives it to persons who from age, disease, accident, and often from their own vice or improvidence, are unable to support themselves. It supports those who, disabled by accident, have failed to get damages from their employers, and perhaps some of those who having succeeded have spent their damages. It is in the last resort an insurer against want, and its losses are paid from public funds through one set of agents, — the public officers,

## REDUCTION OF LITIGATION

whether of state, city or town, who administer poor relief. Can it not make its present contribution through other agents, and perhaps insure against its liability by becoming a party to such a scheme of mutual insurance as I have outlined, with proper safeguards? There would seem to be no constitutional objection to a measure carefully drawn to accomplish this, but if there is, the Constitution may be amended.

Might the State not also require of employers a certain standard of care, and impose penalties for any failure to comply with such requirement, and might not such penalties be used to increase the fund of which I am speaking? The careless employer costs the State in many ways, especially in the cost of courts and poor relief. Can he not be compelled to reimburse the State for this expense, and cannot this reimbursement be used so as to relieve the State from the burden of supporting the victims of his carelessness? To put it in another way,

## REFORM OF LEGAL PROCEDURE

an employer of labor proposes to engage in a business which is likely to entail expense on the State through accident to his employees, which will cause either the expense of lawsuits or the cost of supporting disabled men and their families, and often both. The State can offer the employer the alternative of protecting it against these expenses, either by joining in some scheme of insurance or by paying a heavy tax which could be imposed on all employers as a class who did not insure. Such a law as this must be constitutional.

Much of what has been suggested can be done by contracts between employer and employee and a mutual insurance company of employers, classifying injuries and fixing the sum which the employee shall recover according as his injury belongs to one class or another. The contract may provide, as the Mexican law does, for a regular periodical payment, either for a definite time or pending disability, instead of a single payment. The funds of the organization may be placed

## REDUCTION OF LITIGATION

under State control, its investments may be regulated so as to insure safety, and the State may perhaps agree to contribute. The whole community is of necessity a mutual insurance company, and the burdens which this relation creates may well be adjusted by proper legislation. The tendency everywhere is to make proper provision for age and disability in part at the State's expense.

But employers may refuse to enter such organizations. The remedy is simple. The State, in the exercise of the police power, now regulates factories, bakeries, the hours of labor, prescribes safety appliances, insists that all drugs sold shall conform to certain standards which are subject to more or less frequent change, fixes the quality of milk and food, and legislates in various ways to promote the health and safety of its citizens. It is easy to provide that every employer must take the precautions required by the mutual insurance company under heavy penalties. It may direct that his business may

be stopped until he does so, as the State now forces the owners of buildings to make proper provision against fire. It may make it in this way so much for his advantage to join the organization of employers that he cannot afford not to do so.

To recapitulate briefly, there is money enough spent and wasted by our present system, and directly or indirectly paid by the community, to create a fund adequate under a proper system to give proper compensation to every workman injured in the course of his employment. The more carefully this problem is studied, the more certainly will this appear. What is needed is a plan which will at once reduce the danger of accident, and insure the direct application of what the community pays to the relief of the injured person. Whatever is paid on this account should be distributed as an expense, not of one employer, but at least of all engaged in like business through a system of mutual insurance, and should be regarded as an expense of

## REDUCTION OF LITIGATION

the business which enters into the cost of the goods made or work done by the employer, and so is assessed upon the community. If necessary, the State can well afford to contribute, and the question is how to frame a law which will accomplish our result. It has been done in Germany, to the great relief of the courts, and it should be done here. Let me give you a few facts as to the German system, to be found in the last annual report issued by the United States Bureau of Labor, as condensed by a correspondent of the *Boston Transcript:*

"The employers defray the entire cost of the accident insurance, and it includes practically all the industrial workers in the country. The most striking evidence of the wide scope of this system is contained in the figures for the operations of the year 1908. In this year, the number of persons insured against accident was about 27,000,000, the total receipts were about $57,000,000, the total expenditures were about $48,000,000, and the amount of the reserve was

## REFORM OF LEGAL PROCEDURE

$65,000,000. The number of workmen compensated for the first time in the year 1908 was 143,000. Separate laws provide a system of compulsory sickness insurance for wage-earners in which the employers pay one-third and the workmen two-thirds of the expense. In 1908 the number of persons (not including agricultural laborers) insured against sickness was about 13,000,000, the receipts were $95,000,000, and the expenditures were $91,000,000. Besides these two branches, there is a third national compulsory system relating to insurance for old age and invalidity, in which the employers and the workmen each pay equal amounts while the Imperial Government provides a liberal subsidy. In 1908 the number of persons insured under this branch was 15,000,000, the receipts were $68,000,000, the expenditures were $48,000,000, while the reserve amounted to $355,000,000. The three systems of insurance have been in operation for nearly twenty-five years, and the experience under them has been so favorable that, in response to a widespread demand, the German Government is now preparing to revise and extend the system, and it is expected that in a few years even greater results will be shown than those now obtained. A number of cities in Germany are now providing subsidies for organizations providing benefits in cases of unemployment; this is usually done by repaying the trade unions and similar organizations a percentage of the expenditures they make for out-of-work, travel, etc., benefits."

We cannot afford to treat our workmen worse than Germany treats hers, and some system like hers should be established, and will be established in this country. If any provisions of our constitutions prevent, the difficulty must be removed by amendment. It is largely a question of mathematics, and whenever the facts and figures are laid before the business community, its sound sense will repudiate our present absurdly expensive and ineffectual methods.

REFORM OF LEGAL PROCEDURE

As the Committee on the Judiciary of the National House of Representatives said in a report last year:

"Practically every civilized industrial nation in the world has since discarded the old system based on fault, and submitted a system under which the industry bears the burden of relieving the distress of its injured workers practically without litigation.

"That this question is of transcendent importance and one wholly connected with the advanced policies of· the Government respecting the rights of labor and the proper equitable relations between the employer and the workman, is evidenced by the utterance of President Taft, in a recent address at Worcester, Mass., speaking before the joint committee of brotherhood in train service:

"I am hopeful, indeed, that before many years have passed we shall be able to adopt a system . . . by which there shall be settled promptly, on rules specified with the same degree of certainty

## REDUCTION OF LITIGATION

that they are specified in an insurance policy, how much a man shall receive for an injury, proportionate to the wages that he gets and proportionate to the disabling character of the injury. . . . In other words, I think we ought to have a uniformity of award, a dispatch and quickness in award, so that the lawyers may be eliminated, and that the money may go directly to the object to which it ought to be devoted. It will rid the courts of litigation with which they are now loaded down. It will make the awards reasonable but quick, and there will be no division in the money paid to the widow and the orphans or to the helpless cripple. That system is forcing its way in Europe, and I hope we may have it here. In that way the good feeling between the company and the employee will be facilitated and justice will be done. The railroads can calculate with the utmost accuracy, by statistical reference, how much money they will have to devote to that sort of liability, and I think everybody will be in better

## REFORM OF LEGAL PROCEDURE

condition. The middleman will be eliminated, and only the employee, on the one hand, and the treasury of the railroad, on the other, will be affected.'

"And by President Roosevelt's address at Jamestown:

"As a matter of fact there is no sound economic reason for distinction between accidents caused by negligence and those which are unavoidable, and the law should be such that the payment of those accidents will become automatic instead of being a matter for a lawsuit. Workmen should receive a certain definite and limited compensation for all accidents in industry, irrespective of negligence. It is neither just, expedient, nor humane; it is revolting to judgment and sentiment alike, that the financial burden of accidents occurring because of the necessary exigencies of their daily occupation should be thrust upon the sufferers who are least able to bear it.'"

No man can work out a perfect system, but

## REDUCTION OF LITIGATION

on the general lines which have been suggested, the problem of dealing with the protection of employers from accidents and their consequences can and will be settled, and among other results the courts will be relieved from a certain class of cases. Gentlemen, there is here an opportunity for you all.

But there remain much larger classes which this scheme would not touch. Such are the claims of passengers and others not employees against transportation companies. The first are most easily dealt with in the case of railroads or steamship companies which carry passengers for considerable distances. In their stations the passenger goes to one window and gets the ticket which entitles him to transportation, and at an adjoining window may get another ticket which entitles him to a certain sum in case he is injured by an accident during his journey. For the latter he pays a trifling sum, which includes besides what is needed to cover the risk of loss, something for the expenses and profit of the insurance company. Why should not these be combined, and the railroad company insure its passengers? It does in effect insure them now, and it maintains an expensive legal department to liquidate by costly trials the claims against it as such, to protect itself against fraudulent claims, and perhaps to make men whose claims are just take less than their due rather than incur the risk and expense of litigating with a rich corporation. The Courts have laid down the rule, that a carrier cannot by contract exempt himself from the consequences of his own negligence, but he can limit his liability and give the passenger one liability for one price and less for a less price, or nothing for nothing, as in the case of one who travels on a free pass. Why should not the railroad company add a small sum to the price of its ticket, and for that assume the liability of an insurer, and why should not the passenger who is willing to take the very trifling risk of accident be allowed to do so? A very small sum added to the price of a ticket would

## REDUCTION OF LITIGATION

cover all losses and be for the company's advantage, and this sum could be fixed by a Board of Railroad Commissioners or other representative of the State so as to prevent extortion.

It must be possible to regulate by some reasonable contract the relations between passenger and carrier, so that the passenger may get a greater or less degree of insurance according to the price which he pays without imposing on the railroad a greater burden than it now carries. At present the carrier agrees for a certain price to carry the passenger safely, and in case it fails to do so to pay a sum to be fixed by the Court according to circumstances. Why should not the parties agree upon the sum to be paid and the price be adjusted according to the service performed and the risk assumed by the carrier, as the carrier now varies his price for baggage according to its weight and its character? It would seem to be a problem which is not insoluble, and there is no sound legal reason for refusing parties the right to make such contracts.

When we come to the case of street railways, the difficulty increases. There the journeys are short, the passengers constantly changing, and more careless in getting on and off than on steam cars, and moreover the fare is a fixed sum represented by a single coin or multiples of that coin, and any change in this fare is difficult to arrange. On the other hand the percentage of passengers who are not carried safely is almost infinitesimal. Still the total number of persons carried is so large that an insignificant percentage makes a formidable total of cases from the Court's point of view, and the number of fraudulent claims is larger than with other carriers because the identity of passengers is not easily established, and it may be very difficult to disprove a false story. It might be possible to reduce litigation by a slight extension of the principle which I have suggested in the case of steam railways. The legislature

## REDUCTION OF LITIGATION

might limit to a small sum the liability which the company shall insure by the receipt of a five-cent fare, providing at the same time that if passengers are not willing to take so much risk the Company might issue more expensive tickets, or meet the wants of regular passengers by issuing tickets of insurance covering longer or shorter periods charging for such insurance a reasonable rate. In brief, the Legislature might provide that by the acceptance of a certain fare the company should be held to have assumed a limited liability, and that for any greater liability the passenger must pay. This is perhaps a crude suggestion, but it may lead some one of you to work out a better plan.

The claims of injured persons, who are not passengers and with whom no contract can be made, still remain, but they are comparatively few, and for the present may be left to the Courts, for I would not take all the bread out of your expectant mouths.

All these suggestions, however, are made in

## REFORM OF LEGAL PROCEDURE

support of my main proposition, that the congestion of the dockets and the consequent delay of suitors may be dealt with by legislation, so regulating the subject out of which the disputes grow as to make litigation unnecessary or unprofitable.

But there is left the large class of fraudulent claims brought on speculation, and supported by manufactured, exaggerated or perverted testimony and by professional experts. These cannot always be detected. If they could they would never be brought, but when they are exposed, the punishment should be severe and certain. In dealing with them, the Court and the Bar should act together. The Bar has the right to ask the Court for information, and the Court has the right to ask the Bar for investigation and report. In every considerable section there is, or should be, an association of lawyers to hold up the standard of legal practice, and to purify the Bar. If the Court is satisfied, or has strong reason to suspect, that a case is fraudulent, it

## REDUCTION OF LITIGATION

should notify the representatives of this association and ask them to investigate. There is no tribunal that a tricky attorney dreads more than one composed of his honest associates, and there is no penalty that he fears more than their condemnation. The mere danger, that if his fraud is detected his case will be sent to the Bar Association for investigation, would be a powerful deterrent. Unless a fraud is very glaring, he has now nothing to fear from the loss of a suit except the loss of his time, and some small expenses perhaps. If he knew that the judge stood ready to inform the Bar and the Bar stood ready to investigate, and if he knew further that detection would be followed by swift and inexorable punishment like suspension or disbarment, the amount of improper litigation would be enormously reduced. This is a step to which the profession must come if it would purify the courts and recover its proper standing. It would involve time and trouble to apply this remedy at first, but after two or three examples had been made and the proper standard established, it would not often be necessary to take actual proceedings.

Another step towards discouraging fraudulent suits by striking at the means employed in prosecuting them has been suggested by Samuel Untermyer, the well-known lawyer of New York, who in an address delivered a year ago made this statement:

"It has been said, and I think rightly, that the crime of perjury is committed in at least three out of every five cases tried in the courts in which an issue of fact is involved. It has become so general that the Courts regard it as almost a part of the inevitable accompaniment of a trial."

He suggests that the Court should be obliged, at every trial before a jury, to require the jury to find whether any witness before it has been guilty of wilful false swearing, and if so to name the witness or witnesses. At trials before the Court without a jury, the judge would be required to make this finding. There are many objections

## REDUCTION OF LITIGATION

to this remedy, but if the judge were to watch trials carefully, and wherever perjury was clearly committed to report the case to the prosecuting officer, or even commit the witness to await the action of the Grand Jury, it would have a strong deterrent effect. I have known this done without especial statutory authority, and it is certain that some steps should be taken to purify trials in this matter. A few conspicuous cases would have a very wholesome influence, and all honorable members of the Bar should exert themselves to root out this evil.

Disputed wills are a prolific source of litigation, and in passing I may call your attention to a suggested method of preventing these contests. It is proposed that a statute be passed providing that the testator may, if he pleases, file his will in court during his life and give due notice to all the world, and that if anyone questions its validity on any ground he must appear within a certain time and contest it or be forever barred. If a contestant appears, let him be required to prove his interest, and then under proper restrictions be allowed to see the will. If he still desires to contest it, let the questions which he raises be tried while the testator himself can testify and demonstrate his capacity or explain his reasons. Under such a law, contested will cases would be rare, and yet abundant protection would be afforded against incapacity, fraud, and undue influence. Doubtless many other laws might be suggested which would reduce the volume of litigation, but I wish to leave a large field open for your ingenuity, and will end this branch of my subject here.

## III

### *DELAYS DURING TRIAL*

THUS far I have dealt with the causes of delay before trial, and have suggested as remedies a higher standard of professional fidelity which shall eliminate groundless suits and improper defences, the imposition of substantial costs on client or counsel in proper cases, a keener professional conscience which shall overcome the temptation to procrastinate, and the removal of certain classes of litigation from the courts by legislation.

Let us now proceed to consider those things which prolong the trial itself, or prevent a prompt and just judgment. These can be dealt with more briefly, and we will begin by assuming that the case is tried by jury or Court without first sending it to a master or auditor. Delay can be caused in such a trial only by

## REFORM OF LEGAL PROCEDURE

needlessly prolix examination or cross-examination of witnesses, by sparring between counsel, or, where the hearing is before a judge or judges, by delay in the decision. Where a jury tries the issue there may also be delay in selecting the jurors, but this will be dealt with when we come to consider the administration of criminal law, for in civil cases delay on this account is not common.

The length to which the examination and cross-examination of witnesses shall be pressed, and the extent to which cumulative evidence shall be allowed, must be left to the determination of the presiding judge, who must also control the conduct of counsel during the trial. The first is a matter of discretion, the second, in at least one important respect, should be governed by strict rules. In many trials much time is wasted in altercations between counsel. One lawyer will make a statement of fact or a personal charge against his opponent or some joke at his expense. The other dares not remain silent lest he be thought to admit the fact or the charge, or lose by not answering a joke in kind. When the laugh is against a man, he and his case may suffer with the jury. Hence the lawyer who is attacked replies, and an unseemly dispute ensues, which delays the trial, confuses the jury, and exasperates the combatants, neither of which consequences helps in the ascertainment of justice. The judge can and should stop all such interruptions of orderly proceedings at once, by inexorably requiring counsel to address the Court and not each other. A judge who enforces this rule confers an obligation on every one concerned — on the public, by preventing a waste of public time, on the jury, who are often disgusted and wearied by constant squabbles between counsel, and on the counsel themselves, who are often dragged into such disputes reluctantly lest silence be misinterpreted, and who say things in heat of which in their cooler moments they are thoroughly ashamed. A judge in this matter should be prompt and firm.

## REFORM OF LEGAL PROCEDURE

The Court may well interfere also to prevent a waste of time in examining witnesses. It is true that a cross-examiner should not be compelled to disclose his object, since to do so is often to put a false witness on his guard and so defeat the whole purpose of cross-examination, but a strong and experienced judge can generally tell whether counsel is wasting or merely using time. Even the ablest lawyer, in dealing with a witness, is sometimes carried along by the delight of the contest, and in the attempt to score a personal triumph over the witness loses sight of his case. A little interruption or expression of weariness will bring him to his senses, and an inept counsel can by a hint be persuaded to abandon an unprofitable lead.

Some years ago, a friend of mine in England was watching the trial of a case when one of the counsel called a witness. "Why do you call this witness?" said the judge. "I want to make the jury understand the working of a winch" was the reply. "Oh," said the judge,

## DELAYS DURING TRIAL

"the jury understands that," and turning to the jury, he said: "Gentlemen, don't you all know what a winch is and how it works?" They all nodded assent. "You see," continued the judge, "you don't need this witness. Call your next." A little while later the case was given to the jury, who, as is very often the case in England consulted without leaving the box. After a few minutes the judge turned to them, and said: "Well, gentlemen, have you agreed?" "We stand eleven to one," answered the foreman." Addressing the counsel the judge said: "Gentlemen, will you take the verdict of the eleven?" They assented, and the case was ended. This was practical sense, and it may be added that consultation by the jurymen under the eye of the judge and counsel should be encouraged. It insures attention to business, and avoids much waste of men in the jury-room.

There is another saving of time which is within the control of counsel, who can always avoid prolix and useless examination and cross-

## REFORM OF LEGAL PROCEDURE

examination. Direct examination is really more difficult than cross-examination, and should be prepared carefully. The counsel must learn what the witness knows, and then make him tell his story connectedly and simply, — as far as possible chronologically, avoiding digressions and interruptions of the narrative. Testimony that is not extracted by leading questions is more effective than the responses of a witness who is led, but there are worse faults than leading, which is often necessary with certain witnesses in the interest of reasonable expedition.

Cross-examination is a very dangerous amusement where an honest witness has told the truth and there is no fact within his knowledge which cross-examining counsel needs — a cross-examination only doubles the effect of his testimony, irritates him, and perhaps stimulates his memory to the injury of the cross-examiner. With such a witness, the most effective course is to say: "That is all" or "No questions."

## DELAYS DURING TRIAL

This often disappoints the opponent who has extracted the bare facts and relied on cross-examination to fill in the details. It indicates to the jury that the cross-examiner's case is not injured by the witness, and if a case is well prepared this must be so, since you must have known what the witness would say and have some way of meeting his testimony, else you have no case. Cross-examination is useful in bringing out helpful facts from an honest witness, in making a false witness testify positively to statements which the cross-examiner can contradict, and in breaking a lying witness down by exposing his falsehood, but cross-examination for general results without a definite plan — the Micawber-like process of asking questions in the hope that "something will turn up" — is generally fatal. When a witness has done your case all the harm possible and he must be broken, then, and then only, is such a process to be justified. If counsel would bear these simple rules in mind, much aimless and useless

# REFORM OF LEGAL PROCEDURE

cross-examination would be avoided to the advantage of all concerned.

In this country we are too apt to regard a trial, not as a business-like attempt to settle a question between two parties with the help of court and counsel, but as a battle in the nature of a prize-fight between counsel. Each side is provided with a table, and sits down for a long siege, while every word, however used, is carefully recorded by the stenographers, and the judge sits as an interested spectator with the power of a time-keeper. In England the counsel sit in semi-circular pews, with scant accommodation, and each rises where he sits to examine witnesses or address the jury. This very difference in the seating of counsel typifies the difference in the procedure. The English judge controls the trial from beginning to end and interposes to shorten the proceedings with great freedom, while in America such intervention would be resented. Yet no one complains that the English Courts do not do justice.

## DELAYS DURING TRIAL

It is important, also, that the trial should be so conducted that there will be no second trial of the same facts. This can in many cases be done by submitting to the jury distinct issues of fact or requiring them to answer specific questions, a practice which has been repeatedly recommended by the American Bar Association and other organizations of high standing. As cases are generally submitted to a jury, the jurymen are required, after a long trial and moving appeals to their passions and prejudices, upon evidence which must be remembered imperfectly, and under instructions on complicated questions of law at best imperfectly understood, to decide whether on the whole the plaintiff or the defendant should prevail. The real issues are obscured or forgotten, and a jury must often agree upon a verdict without really considering the vital questions upon which the rights of the parties depend.

For example, some years ago a lawyer arguing

## REFORM OF LEGAL PROCEDURE

for the plaintiff in an accident suit against a railway company, said to the jury: "Gentlemen, my client needs the paltry sum which she seeks to recover at your hands. Oh, *how* she needs it! You have seen her. You have seen her age, her weakness, her inability to struggle with the world. You can judge how this accident has affected her, and how much good this money will do her. And, gentlemen, while I speak to you, — in these few minutes, this great corporation is taking in, at a few of its ticket offices, more money than enough to make her comfortable for life. She needs it, and the defendant does not, — will never miss it. Can you hesitate, gentlemen, between the two?" The judge sat by and heard in silence this appeal. How much attention, do you think, the jury gave to the question of the defendant's negligence or the plaintiff's want of due care? The facts, that one party is a corporation and the other an individual, that one is rich and the other poor, that one is native and the other foreign, that

## DELAYS DURING TRIAL

one is white and the other colored, often outweigh evidence and law.

I remember once defending a corporation against an absurd claim, and the judge began his charge by saying: "Gentlemen of the Jury:— In my years of service on the bench I have seen more injustice done because juries have allowed their minds to be influenced by the fact that one of the parties was a corporation than from any other single cause. Now I want you in this case to ignore this fact, and to decide it as if both plaintiff and defendant were individuals." The jury were out nineteen hours, and then gave me a verdict. An old juryman afterwards came to my office, and said, "You know the judge told us that we mustn't allow the fact that the defendant was a corporation to influence our minds. Well, *finally*, I didn't allow it to influence my mind." This confession shows what goes on in the juryroom.

The way to avoid the influence of these prejudices is to make the jury decide the real issues involved. When the jury is required to answer direct questions, they are forced to consider the real issues of facts, and the verdict settles the facts once for all. The Court can then order a verdict one way or the other, and let the appellate Court, if it does not affirm the ruling, order such a judgment upon the findings as the law requires. The province of the jury is to find facts and assess damages, and to this province they should be limited. If the jury were regularly asked in accident cases such questions as: "Was the defendant negligent?" "If so, in what did the negligence consist": or if the claim is that the plaintiff did not exercise due care by omitting some precaution or doing some careless thing, the judge were to submit the question whether he did do the thing or omit the precaution suggested, the jury would in fact deal with the questions which, in theory, they must decide in order to reach a verdict, but which, in practice, may or may not receive their attention. Were this system adopted, the parties would not be compelled to try the questions of fact again, because the judge at the trial erred in his views of liability upon these facts. One trial would suffice to establish the facts, and a verdict upon them could only be set aside for flagrant errors in omitting or excluding evidence which bore upon these issues.

In dealing with questions of evidence, the Appellate Court should be given liberal discretion to sustain the verdict where it is reasonably apparent that the admitted or excluded evidence ought not to have changed the jury's conclusion, or that the judgment of the Court below was in itself just. Remembering that the trial judge may always set aside an improper verdict, and that the case rarely reaches the Appellate Court until the power has been invoked, the slight chance of injustice arising from an error in dealing with evidence committed both by the trial judge and the Appellate Court is infinitesimal as compared with the injustice done by the present practice,

## REFORM OF LEGAL PROCEDURE

and the delay and expense to which not only the parties but all litigants in the same court are put by repeated new trials.

Let me give two illustrations of existing difficulties taken from a recent article by Mr. George W. Alger. He quotes from the argument of counsel, addressing the New York Court of Appeals in a very uninteresting case about a small plot of land:

(This case has been tried three times in the lower court by juries, has been heard on appeal in this court twice, and once in the Court of Appeals. The expenses of the litigation already have absorbed the value of this property in dispute. If there be some way which the court can find for deciding finally this dispute here in this court, without requiring it to be tried over again, it will be a blessing to all concerned.)

"This blessing the court found itself unable to confer, and six months later the case again was on the first round of the judicial ladder for a

## DELAYS DURING TRIAL

new trial in the lower court; and recently it has been once more decided in the Appellate Court, and is now on its weary way to the Court of Appeals." [1]

Another case which he cites is the case of *Ellis* v. *The Delaware, Lackawanna and Western R. R. Co.*, a suit by a brakeman to recover damages for personal injuries. He was injured in July, 1882, and twenty-two years later he finally recovered judgment for $6500, under the New York system which gives two appeals from the trial court, one to the Appellate Division, and one to the Court of Appeals. During this period, the plaintiff had seven trials of the facts before a jury, and after the first two, the Court of Appeals holding that on his own testimony the trial Court should have directed a verdict for the company, he completely changed his testimony on all points which the Court of Appeals had relied on in reaching its judgment,

---

[1] "Treadmill Justice," *Atlantic Monthly*, vol. 104, November, 1909.

and on this reconstructed case, after eleven years of fresh litigation, he won his final verdict.

This is not an unusual case, for the Court of Appeals has itself said, that "It frequently happens that cases appear and reappear in this court, after three or four trials, where the plaintiff on *every trial* has changed his testimony in order to meet the varying fortunes of the case upon appeal." We may well say, slightly changing a familiar quotation: "Oh, justice, justice! what crimes are committed in thy name!"

Mr. Alger thinks that the expense of this litigation, not including lawyers' fees, was five thousand dollars at a conservative estimate. What it cost either lawyers or clients for the time that the counsel gave is a matter of pure conjecture, but it is safe to say that this litigation profited no one and cost the community dear.

Let me quote one more case from Mr. Alger: "A grimly humorous illustration of one of the

## DELAYS DURING TRIAL

results to the litigant may be found in another New York law-suit which reached a final chapter recently in the Court of Appeals. It was a complex case against an insurance company on some policies of insurance, and each time it was tried it took from a week to two weeks' attention of Court and jury. Owing to reversals and new trials ordered by appellate courts, it had to be tried nine times. It was in the courts from 1882 to 1902. The plaintiff became at last so sick and disheartened with his interminable law-suit that he abandoned it; refused to go to his lawyers to consult with them about it or to appear when the case was being tried. The lawyers had themselves spent over forty-five hundred dollars in fighting the case, and had worked on it for nearly twenty years. Their client having abandoned them, they settled the case for thirty thousand dollars, and took the money themselves for their fees. The last chapter of the litigation was an unsuccessful attempt by the receiver in insolvency of the plaintiff to make the lawyers give up some of their fees to their client's creditors. How much the twenty years' delay in the lawsuit had to do with that insolvency it is impossible to say; but such an outcome, to the lay mind, seems hardly satisfactory as a result of twenty years of litigation, of nine trials, and seventy-two days' time of over a hundred jurors."

These are fruits of the existing system in the richest state of the Union, a great commercial community, old and highly civilized according to our standards. Mr. Alger does well when he says that one great defect in our system is the "lack of terminal facilities."

In Philadelphia, on the 4th of last June, the statement was made by a Mr. Scoville, a member of its Bar, that it usually took two years to reach a jury, while in Pittsburg, in 1909, the number of jury cases waiting trial was 7274 and its four courts had only tried 783 in a year. He quotes from business men such statements as these: "Not being immortal we have decided to bring no more suits in Philadelphia," and "I can obtain justice in hell quicker than in Philadelphia," while a Russian emigrant wrote: "Such denial of justice is misery and despotism. Court conditions in Russia are not as bad as they are here."

Contrast this with what I read in the London "Times," on July 26 last, in an article discussing a proposition to appoint two new judges:

"They will find plenty of work to do, and no small arrears to be cleared off, cases entered *about March last* being still undisposed of."

Much of this interminable delay would be saved if the jury answered specific questions, and the courts merely applied the law to their findings, entering judgment accordingly, with no new trial of facts whenever the trial judge makes a mistake of law.

We wish to minimize the danger of error in the trial court and to insure just findings by the jury as well as correct rulings by the Court. To this end the judge should be allowed to charge the jury on the facts, and not as is now the case in many jurisdictions, forbidden to give the jury any idea of his opinion.

The judge is the only person in court at once trained to apply the law, experienced in trials, and impartial. He is familiar with the wiles of witnesses and counsel, for no man can preside in court for any length of time without learning to detect the evidences of falsehood and to weigh at their true value appeals to prejudice and sympathy. The jury needs all the advice and help that he alone can give them, for as a rule they are entirely without experience in the work which they are asked to do. I have often thought when I have been engaged in discussing with opposing counsel some case which bristled with questions of fact and law, and looking out of the window have seen a miscellaneous crowd listening to some patent medicine-vendor, or watching the moving of a safe, how strange it would sound to a foreigner if he heard me say to my opponent: "We with all our knowledge and experience cannot agree upon this case. Let us take twelve men at random from that crowd and let them decide it." Yet that is what we do in practice, where we let a jury decide without the help of a judge, and the more we limit the judges' power the nearer we come to such an absurdity.

The law of England gives the judge his proper place as the Court, and trial by jury would have been abandoned long ago if this had not been so. I have already alluded to the Tichborne case, in which after the trial had lasted one hundred and sixty-nine days, Chief Justice Cockburn charged the jury for eighteen days, and from his summing up I quote the following words:

"I cannot invent facts, nor by the utmost effort of ingenuity can I find explanations which have no reality in point of fact. In my opinion a judge does not discharge his duty who contents himself with being a mere recipient of evidence, which he is afterwards to reproduce to the jury without pointing out the facts, and the inferences to which they naturally and legitimately give rise. It is the business of the judge so to adjust the scales of the balance that they hang evenly; but it is his duty to see that the facts, as they arise, are placed in the one scale or the other, according as they belong in one or the other. It is his business to take care that the evidence which properly arises from the facts is submitted to the consideration of the jury, with the happy consciousness that, if he goes wrong, there is the judgment of twelve men, experienced in the everyday concerns of life, to set right anything in respect of which he may have erred. If the facts make one scale kick the beam, it is the fault of the facts, not of the judge."

In the Federal Courts this ideal is maintained. "Trial by jury," said Mr. Justice Gray, "in the Courts of the United States, is a trial presided over by a judge, with authority not only to rule upon objections to evidence and to instruct the jury upon the law, but also, when in his judgment the due administration of justice requires it, to aid the jury by explaining and commenting upon and even giving them his opinion upon questions of fact, provided only he submits those questions to their determination." Mr. Justice Brewer states the rule thus: "The judge is primarily responsible for the just outcome of the trial. He is not a mere moderator of a town meeting, submitting questions to the jury for determination, nor simply ruling on the admissibility of testimony, but one who in our jurisprudence stands charged with full responsibility. He has the same opportunity that jurors have for seeing the witnesses, for noting all those matters in a trial not capable of record, and when, in his deliberate opinion, there is no excuse for a verdict save in favor of one party, and he so rules by instructions to that effect, an appellate court will pay large respect to his judgment."[1]

In a word, the judge has, as he should have,

[1] Palton v. Texas & Pacific Ry. Co. 179 U. S. p. 660.

## REFORM OF LEGAL PROCEDURE

a powerful influence on the result. It is not believed that suitors get less justice in the Federal Courts on this account.

In the states, on the other hand, the whole tendency is to reduce the judge's influence and to increase not so much the power of the jury as the power of the skillful advocate upon the result of the trial. This is wholly wrong. Counsel may make every appeal to sympathy and prejudices, and every ingenious attempt to mislead the jurymen, but the judge, who has no reason to mislead them, and who must be more impartial than either counsel, is in many states prevented from saying anything to counteract these improper influences. He is given power to set aside a verdict which in his judgment is wrong, and thus subject the parties to the expense and delay of a second trial, but he can do nothing to secure a true verdict, and that influence which should be most potent in securing a proper result is thus shorn of its power. He may make mistakes in ruling upon

## DELAYS DURING TRIAL

questions of evidence or in his instructions to the jury, and the chance of his doing so lends a permanent element of uncertainty to all trials. From such mistakes come frequent retrials and consequent delay and expense, but as trials are generally conducted, his opportunities for error are numerous, his power to secure justice is slight. We need in our trial courts good judges of high character and sufficient firmness and we must give them more power. We profess the greatest respect for and confidence in the Bench, and express it on every public occasion. As a rule, the Bench deserves this confidence, but in practice we do not trust the men whom we thus delight to honor.

I have said that the tendency is to limit the power of the judge. The reason is, perhaps, that the Bar is represented in the legislature and the Bench is not. The lawyer who feels aggrieved by the action of a judge in some particular case, who has felt the halter draw around his profes-

## REFORM OF LEGAL PROCEDURE

sional neck with the proverbial result, induces other lawyers to unite with him in having a law passed to diminish the judge's power. He and his friends represent one side, no one represents the other, and so the law is passed. As Professor Pound says:

"Legislation with respect to the charge of the Court may be shown to have originated in more than one jurisdiction in the desire of eloquent counsel of a by-gone type to deprive not merely the trial judge but the law, of all influence upon trials, and to leave everything to be disposed of on the arguments."

Unhappily the counsel so described are not wholly "bygone," and in at least one state of my acquaintance there exists an organization of lawyers principally concerned in personal injury cases, which systematically endeavors to obtain legislation that shall remove every obstruction which the judge can interpose between them and the results which they seek.

The practical results would be ludicrous if

## DELAYS DURING TRIAL

they were not so disastrous. Let me give you some specimens.

In some jurisdictions the judge is allowed only to give or refuse written requests for rulings submitted by counsel and is forbidden to say anything else to the jury. The judge must read these requests before the argument, and as a result, when counsel begins to close, he leaves the Bench and impanels another jury, letting counsel argue unchecked. It is difficult to say what may not happen where such license is allowed.

In Iowa and in North Carolina statutes provide that the Court shall not limit the time of any attorney addressing a jury. What is possible where no limit is allowed may be inferred from the fact that before a limitation was imposed in Massachusetts one counsel argued seventeen hours and his opponent eighteen hours in an ordinary case, while some years ago in Delaware the Court gave a week to the hearing of a case which in the Supreme Court of the United States would have taken four hours, and the counsel spent their time while I was present in reading passages from decisions, while the judges were naturally somnolent. Mere sympathy for the Court and jury should forbid such barbarous practices.

The judge's right to see that what happened at the trial is properly stated in the bill of exceptions is not even secured, for in Texas a law provides that if a judge refuses to sign such a bill "it shall be lawful for any two attorneys who may be present at the time to sign such bill of exceptions, which shall have the same force and effect as if signed by the judge."

Another statute, fortunately of brief existence, forbade a judge to require counsel to stand during the examination of witnesses. The genesis of this statute was thus imagined by Mr. Justice Brown, late of the Supreme Court.

"Counsel while examining a witness is sitting rummaging over papers, or otherwise wasting the time of Court and jury. The trial bids fair to

## DELAYS DURING TRIAL

become interminable, the patience of the judge is exhausted, and he orders counsel to rise and give his whole attention to the witness. Counsel is beaten, and smarting under his defeat rushes to the legislature, of which he is perhaps a member, with a proposition to "sit down" upon a judge who takes on such airs. The legislature, in a burst of sympathy passes the act — counsel is avenged and the judge for the time being is squelched."

The act was repealed in just one year from its passage.

And finally the Constitution of Nebraska provides that "the right to be heard in the Supreme Court on error or appeal shall not be denied," a provision which compelled the Supreme Court of Nebraska after three trials to hear a case involving 28 cents.

Mr. Pound well says: "The individual gets so much fair play that the public gets very little."

The whole tendency and object of such legislation is to make the brilliant advocate master of the Court to the manifest impairment of justice, and to give the rich litigant who can pay such an advocate an enormous advantage. The Bar should organize to oppose all such laws and to make the judge a controlling force, and not "a mere umpire" compelled "to sit quietly by and see a manifest wrong done simply because young or inexperienced counsel have overlooked or misapprehended a vital point" — to borrow the words of Mr. Justice Brown. As it is, says Mr. Pound, "The trial judge, without the commanding position which the common law contemplates, hampered by legislative restrictions, and held in check by reviewing tribunals removed from his difficulties, is driven to a cautious, timid, dilatory course, which does not comport with the requirements of business-like administration of justice."

The unwillingness to let the judge charge the jury on facts, for fear that he may influence them unduly, is the more absurd when we remember that in the most complicated and important

## DELAYS DURING TRIAL

matters the judge himself *decides* the facts. All the cases which arise in admiralty, where the amounts involved are sometimes very large, are decided by the judge alone. In equity, where we find such cases as the suits to dissolve the Standard Oil Trust, and the patent causes which involve millions of dollars and affect us all more or less, to say nothing of numberless suits in which the public is less interested but in which issues of great importance to the parties are tried, the judge, or often a lawyer appointed by the judge to act as master, determines the facts. Most of the questions which arise under the Bankrupt law are decided by judges or referees, and I need merely allude to the questions of fact which The Interstate Commerce Commission or Railroad Commissions and like bodies determine. Is it not ridiculous that while we give judges sitting alone such powers, we will not trust them to help a jury determine a question of fact in the pettiest case that is tried before them?

## REFORM OF LEGAL PROCEDURE

The jury, which settles the facts, acts upon evidence which it must remember more or less imperfectly; the counsel who argue the case, the judge who presides, and the Appellate Court which reviews, have a stenographic report of all that is important. A juryman fresh from service asked me whether provision could not be made for giving the jury the same help. Men's memories, after a trial lasting several days or very likely weeks, will certainly differ as to what the testimony of a witness was, and differing recollections as to the words of an important conversation perhaps may determine a case, or at least lead to long discussion between men unused to argument. There may be practical difficulties in the way of sending the stenographer's report to the jury, though these are probably, in large part imaginary, and it would involve more trouble and expense, but it could be left to the judge in any case whether it should be done. The failure to give the jurors this help, which the lawyers and the

## DELAYS DURING TRIAL

courts need, however, emphasizes the importance of giving the jury the benefit of a clear and impartial summing up, pointing out the questions and discussing the evidence. The people of England, where this has always been done, are satisfied. There is no reason why it should not be equally satisfactory in this country. If we cannot trust our judges with this power, we must get judges whom we can trust, and pay what is necessary to command their services. The price is a fixed tenure, independence, adequate powers, and a proper salary, but I will discuss this question more fully hereafter.

Thus far I have been dealing with the delays arising when a case is tried before judge or jury. There are, however, many cases which have to go through a process of sifting before they reach this stage. These are cases at law or in equity involving questions of account or a long investigation of disputed facts, which for that reason are sent for preliminary examination to a person appointed by the court to hear the case and report the facts and his findings. In equity, the report of a master has the same weight as the verdict of a jury in establishing facts, and while his findings may be reviewed by the Court, there is a strong presumption in their favor. In other cases, the report has less probative force but may make a *prima facie* case for the party in whose favor the magistrate finds. Again, as in the courts of the United States, cases are sent to an examiner who takes the testimony of the witnesses and reports the evidence to the Court with no conclusion of his own. The cases in which a master, auditor, or like officer is appointed to find facts or take evidence, are, as a rule, the most important and difficult cases which come before the courts. They involve the largest amounts, and often questions of the greatest public importance, and for every reason a prompt decision is important. Yet it is in just this class of proceeding that delay and expense reach their maximum.

## DELAYS DURING TRIAL

Courts and counsel are alike responsible for the existing abuses, and the cause is generally pure laziness. A long hearing interferes with the docket of a court, and with the daily business of counsel. It is much easier for a judge to act on the conclusions of some one else than to hear testimony, examine accounts, weigh evidence and reach his own conclusions. It is much easier for counsel to put a long case over to some uncertain time when it can be taken up conveniently. A case once begun in court must proceed without interruption to the end, while a case before a master may be broken off, or hearings assigned for a given day may be postponed, whenever the convenience of counsel or magistrate suggests it. A case before a master, in short, is something to be taken up when neither master nor counsel have anything else more important, or perhaps more agreeable, to do. After a long interruption, time is necessarily wasted both before and at the renewed hearing in picking up the lost threads, a process which must involve expense either to counsel or client. The more important the case, the more lawyers employed, the more eminent the counsel and the magistrate, the greater the difficulty in finding the time during a busy year when all are able and willing to attend a hearing. The delays in such cases, therefore, are sometimes appalling, and if a lawyer has a bad case which he does not want to try, the chance of wearying or worrying an adversary into settlement is very great. To get a case sent to a master often means victory, for in that field a Fabius may well conquer a Hannibal.

In the hands of unscrupulous counsel, moreover, this procedure may become a potent means of levying blackmail. Witnesses may be examined day after day for weeks at a time, called upon to search for and produce books and papers which have long been forgotten, exposed to charges of deliberate destruction or concealment in case some document called for has been destroyed or lost, and harassed in every manner which the

## DELAYS DURING TRIAL

experience and skill of counsel can suggest. The witness may be taken from important business at great cost and risk to his or others' affairs, he may be and generally is unused to the sneers and innuendoes in which counsel too frequently indulge, and the mental strain to which the process exposes him is as genuine torture as any inflicted by the boot or the rack, and as well calculated to overcome the power of resisting even an unjust demand. I have known a witness examined for six weeks, from day to day, and dying under the strain when the examination was only half concluded, and any lawyer of large practice can recall instances, perhaps not as extreme, but only less so. The motive of the counsel may be entirely good. He may feel that his client's interest demands such measures or he may not, but the effect on the witness is the same.

Were the trial in court, the witness in such a case would be protected. No such prolonged examination would be permitted, for the judge would interfere and shorten the process, but a master or an auditor, though clothed with the power to exclude evidence or stop examination, is naturally and justly reluctant to exercise this power strictly. He may have a decided opinion as to the law, or as to the value of evidence, but when that opinion is questioned by counsel, he remembers that he is only preparing the case for the Court and that the Court may not agree with him. He feels that it is his duty to let the Court have the means of passing on any point which counsel wish to argue, and therefore to put the record in such form as to present all that either counsel considers important to the decision of every question which is raised. He has nominal power to regulate the hearing, but practically he can only suggest and make rulings for the record. If his authority is disregarded, he may ask the Court to enforce it, but an application to the Court is not pleasant; it is difficult to reproduce in court the situation before the master, and hence the Court is rarely asked to intervene.

## DELAYS DURING TRIAL

If the magistrate is an examiner appointed to take evidence, he has no authority to exclude anything, but can only see that the scribe or stenographer records correctly all that is said, either by witness or counsel. Whether the evidence is competent or flagrantly incompetent, whether the objections of counsel are unnecessarily verbose and vexatious, or entirely proper, they must be written out, and the result is often a mass of irrelevant matter collected at great expense of time and money, and disregarded alike by Court and counsel.

I have taken testimony in a railroad case from Boston to Mobile and in various intermediate cities, occupying the time of a master, some seven counsel, and various stenographers, for five or six months, and it was afterwards printed. The whole enterprise involved very large expense to the parties, yet not one word of that testimony was considered by the Court which heard the case, for it ruled that the plaintiff had no standing to present his claim.

## REFORM OF LEGAL PROCEDURE

The following statement by Judge Hough of New York, made in deciding an important patent suit, will be found in a recent volume of reports:

"*Note.* — It is a duty not to let pass this opportunity of protesting against the methods of taking and printing testimony in equity, current in this circuit (and probably others), excused, if not justified, by the rules of the Supreme Court, especially to be found in patent causes and flagrantly exemplified in this litigation. As long as the Bar prefers to adduce evidence by written depositions, rather than *viva voce* before an authoritative judicial officer, I fear that the antiquated rules will remain unchanged, and expensive prolixity remain the best-known characteristic of equity. But reforms sometimes begin with the contemplation of horrible examples, and it is therefore noted that the records in these cases, as printed, bound, and submitted, comprise 36 large octavo volumes, of which more than one-half contain only repeated

## DELAYS DURING TRIAL

matter, *i.e.*, identical depositions, with changed captions, and exhibits offered in more than one case. In reading the testimony of one side in one set of cases, there were counted over 100 printed pages recording squabbles (not unaccompanied with apparent personal rancor) concerning adjournments; and after arriving at this number it seemed unnecessary to count further. In many parts of the record there are not five consecutive pages of testimony to be found without encountering objections stated at outrageous length, which may serve to annoy and disconcert the witness, but are not of enough vitality to merit discussion in 2,000 pages of briefs. Naturally tempers give way under such ill-arranged procedure, and this record contains language, uncalled for and unjustifiable, from the retort discourteous to the lie direct. And all this lumbers up the court record-room, while clients pay for it! Even when evidence in equity was taken by written answers to carefully drawn interrogatories, the practice was not marked by economy or celerity; but stenography and typewriting, the phonograph and linotype, have become common since our rules were framed, have made compression and brevity old-fashioned, increased expense, and often swamped Bench and Bar alike by the quantity, rather than the quality, of the material offered for consideration. Motions to expunge and limit cross-examination should have been made in these cases, though they are feeble remedies, exposing counsel to personal reproach, and rendering judges afraid of keeping out evidence what they cannot (on motion, at all events) understand. But the radical difficulty, of which this case is a striking (though not singular) example, will remain as long as testimony is without any authoritative judicial officer present, and responsible for the maintenance of discipline and the reception or exclusion of testimony."

When we consider that the method of taking evidence which Judge Hough so strongly condemns is the method prescribed by the rules of

## DELAYS DURING TRIAL

the Federal Courts in equity suits, that in this way are tried the most important cases which engage the attention of those courts, such as the suits to dissolve the great trusts, the suits over the sewing machine, the telephone, and all other patents, to say nothing of other suits involving the vital interests of the parties and often of public importance, we may begin to appreciate the formidable obstacles which confront the unhappy litigant who is obliged to assert or defend his rights in an equity suit brought in the courts of the United States. I cannot see how any but a very rich man or combination of men can afford to assert or deny rights under a patent, or how a poor patentee can obtain justice against a rich infringer. Such a system in an enlightened age and country like our own is intolerable.

The proceedings before masters, auditors, examiners, and similar officers bearing different names in different jurisdictions, are prolific sources of delay, expense, and such other evils as I have pointed out, for two principal reasons.

## REFORM OF LEGAL PROCEDURE

The first is the uncertainty as to when the case will be tried; the second is the waste of time and money expended in trying immaterial issues, in hearing incompetent evidence, and in altercations between counsel whose feelings are strongly enlisted and whose expressions are not controlled by any tribunal which they fear to offend.

The remedy is to cut down the function of these officers as much as possible, and to insure a prompt hearing of cases which are committed to them. For example, the Court before sending a case to a master should hear the parties and decide such questions as it can without a master's assistance. It should define the issues committed to the master, and instruct him as to how they should be tried as far as possible. The Court should insist on such a hearing, whether counsel agree to a reference or not, and in many cases it would become evident that the Court could deal with the whole case more expeditiously and satisfactorily without a master. For example, an eminent judge in my own state told

## DELAYS DURING TRIAL

me recently that two counsel came before him with a motion that a case be referred to a master, both sides agreeing that it was necessary. He made some inquiry as to the nature of the dispute and the time likely to be consumed in hearing the case. The answer to the last question was "Two weeks." "I will hear the case," he said, and as he said it he noticed that the faces of both counsel dropped. They were called upon to face at once a trial which they had hoped to postpone. He did hear it in two days, and the dispute between the parties was thus settled promptly instead of dragging along for months, and perhaps years. There can be no doubt that a scrutiny by the Court of every case before it is committed to a master would largely reduce the amount of work now confided to such officers.

So in dealing with cases now sent to examiners, whose only function is to report the evidence taken before them. The rule should be that all suits should be heard by the Court itself. It involves less labor and insures better results.

## REFORM OF LEGAL PROCEDURE

The labor will be less, because the Court now must read all the evidence, material and immaterial, and it takes little more time to hear than to read what a witness says. If only material testimony were heard and immaterial excluded, the total bulk of testimony would be reduced and time saved, while much wrangling which now interrupts the proceedings would be avoided. The results will be better, because the judge who hears a witness can weigh the value of his testimony much better than when he simply reads it. The delay in answering, the troubled expression, the change of color, the embarrassed manner, which are apparent to the eye and are often convincing proof of falsehood, are not preserved in the printed record, and a reply over which a witness has hesitated for some time reads as if given promptly and clearly. The words alone appear, and they are often the least valuable part of the witness's evidence. How often have you met some worthless beggar in the street who has told you some pathetic tale of misfortune and want. If his words were printed they would touch the heart of any reader, but you who see the watery eye, and smell the breath of the speaker, know perfectly well that he does not deserve help, and that any alms you might give him would be worse than wasted. This truth is recognized by every man who ever tried a case, and appellate tribunals in dealing with the decisions of juries or trial courts constantly give greater weight to their conclusions because they saw and heard the witnesses. It is very unfortunate that these aids to a just decision are so largely denied to litigants in the courts of the United States and all other courts which decide on a written report of the evidence.

Were the rule adopted that the Court itself should hear the evidence, the tribunal called upon to try a suit in equity would first hear the parties and ascertain the character of the evidence to be relied upon. Counsel could be called upon to state whether he had any witnesses that could not be present at the trial, and why. The Court could then decide what testimony should be taken by deposition, and within what time, bearing in mind that, as a rule, the witness can be brought to the tribunal more easily and cheaply than the examiner and counsel can be carried to the witness. The work of the examiner can in this way be much curtailed without increasing the Court's labors and with great advantage to the parties. To have one magistrate hear and report and another read and decide is in many cases an unnecessary duplication of labor.

To secure a prompt trial before master or auditor the hearings before them should not be left to the convenience of counsel. The amount of important work now confided to such judicial officers is sufficient to justify the creation of regular tribunals to do this work. To-day there are certain lawyers who are much employed as auditors and masters, and many others who are employed occasionally. They are poorly paid, they can never be sure that the days which they

## DELAYS DURING TRIAL

appoint for hearings will not be lost because counsel at the last moment decide to postpone, and there is therefore danger that the work will fall into the hands of men whose time is not very valuable, especially as busier men find it harder to waste time. There are some who seek such employment at the hands of their friends, and who, desiring more, cannot help respecting the hand that feeds them. As the Court generally asks the parties to agree upon the man, there is almost always a struggle between counsel to select some one who from temperament or association is at least certain not to favor the other side. In a word, the whole system is opposed to the fundamental principle which was well stated by high authority in these words: "The tribunal should always wait the case, not the case the tribunal." In other words, an impartial and competent court or magistrate should be created to try all cases that arise, and not a special tribunal be selected by the contending parties for a particular case. A permanent court follows fixed rules of law, and avoids making bad precedents. The special tribunal only settles the dispute before it, and often takes a short cut across the law to reach its conclusion. Referees are apt "to split the difference."

In any jurisdiction where there is enough work there should be permanent auditors or masters adequately paid and able to regulate and enforce the attendance of parties before them. They should stand as courts, and trials before them should proceed from day to day as in courts, except for good cause shown. It should not be possible to turn the parties out of court because their case is difficult and sure to occupy much time, without taking adequate measures to secure prompt action from the tribunal to which the burden of dealing with their dispute is transferred. The present system is indefensible. To apply the remedies which I have suggested we must have able, strong, and courageous judges. Without these no courts can succeed.

## DELAYS DURING TRIAL

Indeed, the suggestion that before sending a case to a master or auditor the Court have a preliminary hearing, and decide all questions which it can without the aid of such an officer, might well be extended. If there were a judge before whom either counsel in a case might summon his opponent with a view of determining what the real questions at issue were and providing for their prompt determination, much time would be saved to courts and parties. A justice sitting on the Supreme Bench of the United States, and of large judicial experience before he became a member of that tribunal, once said to me in speaking of cases heard before it: "They are generally decided at the argument. It is said that in battle the opposing lines rarely cross bayonets, for before they meet one or the other gives way. So in court, one or the other side so clearly preponderates at the argument that the decision is easy."

A wise and experienced judge trying to ascertain the real question between the parties in a

## REFORM OF LEGAL PROCEDURE

case, and upon what theories of fact and law each was proceeding, could clear away a great deal of rubbish, could make the case easier for the Court to try, could determine the issues, and how they should be tried, could point out their errors to counsel, and in many cases could bring about a settlement, for a very large proportion of litigants would yield to his advice.

This is not mere theory. The plan has been adopted in the English Courts which, by a series of rules, has made it possible for counsel to summon his opponent before a judge and upon a proper showing secure directions which speed the cause. Let me read you specimens of these rules.

380. "Where in any cause or matter it appears to the Court or a judge that the issues of fact in dispute are not sufficiently defined, the parties may be directed to prepare issues, and such issues shall, if the parties differ, be settled by the Court or a judge.

381. "The Court or a judge may, at any stage

## DELAYS DURING TRIAL

of the proceedings in a cause or matter, direct any necessary inquiries or accounts to be made or taken, notwithstanding that it may appear that there is some special or further relief sought for or some special issue to be tried, as to which it may be proper that the cause or matter should proceed in the ordinary manner.

657a. "Whenever an application shall be made before trial for an injunction or other order, and on the opening of such application, or at any time during the hearing thereof, it shall appear to the judge that the matter in controversy in the cause or matter is one which can be most conveniently dealt with by an early trial, without first going into the whole merits on affidavit or other evidence for the purposes of the application, it shall be lawful for the judge to make an order for such trial accordingly, and to direct such trial to be held at the next or any other assizes for any place, if from local or other circumstances it shall appear to him to be convenient so to do, and in the meantime to make such order as the justice of the case may require.

967. "A Court or a judge shall have power to enlarge or abridge the time appointed by these rules, or fixed by any order enlarging time, for doing any act or taking any proceeding, upon such terms (if any) as the justice of the case may require, and any such enlargement may be ordered, although the application for the same is not made until after the expiration of the time appointed or allowed."

Such able and experienced lawyers as alone are appointed to the English Bench, when brought into direct and somewhat informal contact with counsel, can boil the case down and often dispose of it entirely in a comparatively short hearing. It would surprise the members of our Bar to see the Privy Council, or a County Court, simplify a case and expedite the hearing.

# IV

### *DELAY IN APPELLATE COURTS*

THUS far I have dealt with the delays which beset the path of the suitor before he gets his first decision. This unhappily is too often only a beginning. There is still before him a long vista of appeals, and possible new trials. May I give you an illustration of what is possible. A Borough President, in New York, summarily removed a chief of bureau, and the latter questioned his power to do it without a hearing. One would say that the question was simple and that it should be determined at once. Yet the case which the removed officer brought to test the question had forty-seven hearings at Special Terms of the Supreme Court, twenty-one hearings at trial terms, eight appeals were heard and decided

## REFORM OF LEGAL PROCEDURE

in the Appellate Division, and two in the Court of Appeals. At the end of six years three unheard appeals were pending, and $38,000 of back salary depended on the final decision, while the cost of the litigation to the taxpayers was even more. I take these facts from the New York newspapers, but I spare you their indignant and wholly just reflections upon such an exhibition of the law's incompetency.

Again, the Franchise Tax law of New York was passed in 1899. It was held constitutional by every court of New York and by the Supreme Court of the United States. Nearly five years later, two-thirds of the tax for ten years was still unpaid, and the public service corporations were still litigating about the assessment. New York saw before it an indefinite vista of delay, yet taxes should be collected promptly.

No wonder the Committee appointed by the Association of the Bar of the City of New York in a report to that body says:

"Many experienced judges claim that our

## DELAY IN APPELLATE COURTS

system of practice has developed into an appellate system based upon the fundamental idea that the trial and decision are presumptively wrong. . . . Instead of a system of single trials with a minority of reversals on the merits, as in jurisdictions which have modernized their practice, a system of several trials of almost every important case, resulting from technical reversals not affecting the merits, has arisen . . . making the law a game rather than a science."

And they quote Justice O'Gorman, the new senator from New York, who says:

"One of the gravest faults with our present mode of trial is the ease and frequency with which judgments are reversed on technicalities which do not effect the merits of the case and which at no stage have affected the merits."

Can you have a severer indictment than this of Courts which presumably sit to do justice? In striving for perfection in matters immaterial, what is material is forgotten, and justice is ignored.

## REFORM OF LEGAL PROCEDURE

The English Court of Appeals, on an average, grants only twelve new trials a year, and these upon the merits.

It justifies the words of Lord Justice Bowen spoken more than twenty years ago. "It may be asserted without fear of contradiction that it is not possible in the year 1887 for an honest litigant in Her Majesty's Supreme Court to be defeated by any mere technicality, any slip, any mistaken step in his litigation." Cannot we do what the English have done?

The rule should be that from the trial Court there should be an appeal to a bench of judges, but only one appeal. A citizen has the right to a trial of his case, and to a review of the proceedings at the trial by a tribunal of competent lawyers. This is necessary, that the law may be kept uniform, and that a man's rights may not depend on decisions made hastily in the heat of a trial. The law under which the community lives should be settled after cool deliberation. We should take pains to make the tribunal to which this task is confided competent in every way, but when this has been done nothing is gained by giving the parties another hearing before another appellate court. The first may of course make mistakes, but so may the second. It is in most cases more important that the law should be settled than how it is settled. Men accommodate themselves to any fixed rule of conduct, and very bad errors are soon corrected by the court which makes them.

The theory is that a final court of great and perhaps more highly paid lawyers is more reliable. Then why have the intermediate appeal? Some bench of lawyers must finally settle the law in each jurisdiction, so far as the courts can settle it. Why not have one such court and make it as good as the lot of humanity will permit, rather than establish a poor court to make errors for the good court to correct. Lawyers may and do differ as well as doctors, but the highest court is always right because it is the highest. Nothing can destroy the layman's confidence in the law more than to have one bench of lawyers overrule another. It is better and cheaper to have only one appellate court and make that worthy of public confidence. Were this rule adopted, the delays arising from successive appeals now possible in many states would be avoided.

To this rule there is one exception. Every citizen of the United States lives under two systems of law. The State courts administer one system, the Federal courts another, and on many questions the rules established by the two tribunals differ in the same state. Not only this, but the laws of the different states vary widely in many respects, and hence the importance of the very common question whether in a given situation the *lex loci contractus* or the *lex fori* shall govern, and of other questions arising from the conflict of laws. So far as the differences between the laws of the states are concerned, these are best dealt with by uniform legislation, and for many years the American Bar Association

## DELAY IN APPELLATE COURTS

has been laboring to promote this uniformity in many matters with great success. The states learn readily from each other, and a new law adopted by one is soon copied by others, as the Australian ballot law went from state to state.

As between the Federal and the State courts in the same state, the differences also must be dealt with by legislation in most cases, and here uniformity is most desirable. To-day, a man's rights may change as often as he crosses the boundary of a state, or if he remains at home he may find one law, if his case is tried in the State court, and another, if it is removed to a court of the United States. Upon identical facts, he may owe one duty to his fellow-citizen and another to a foreigner.

It would be a great blessing to the people of this country if they could live under uniform laws, if the status of husband and wife, the law of marriage and divorce, statutes regulating corporations and the rights and liabilities of their stockholders, the statute of limitations

## REFORM OF LEGAL PROCEDURE

and the methods of assessing and collecting taxes were uniform, or properly accommodated to each other. To-day the laws which fix inheritance and transfer taxes are so numerous and ill-assorted that a man is driven more and more to invest his money in his own state rather than run the risk of paying two, three, or four inheritance taxes on the same investment, and in time it will be found that the free passage of capital from state to state, so essential to the development of this country, will be seriously hampered to the disadvantage of us all. It has been well said that, to-day, a man cannot afford to die. If you think that four taxes on one investment is an instance of tropical imagination, let me set you right. A lady dies in California. She is the beneficiary under a Massachusetts trust, and the trustees resident in Massachusetts have invested in the stocks of Illinois or New York corporations. She has power to dispose of the trust property by will, and does so. California claims a tax because she resided there, New York and Illinois because shares in their corporations passed in those states, Massachusetts because the trust property passed there, and the United States its tax on the whole. This medley of conflicting laws must be dealt with by lawyers and the legislatures of the states, and when you are members of these bodies you may well bear in mind this situation, and help your profession and your country by trying to improve it.

But the interpretation of the law when passed should be uniform, and for that reason the suggestion that there should be only one appeal in each case will not apply in cases which arise under the constitution and laws of the United States. It is necessary that there should be an intermediate appellate court, like the Circuit Court of Appeals, to deal finally with perhaps most of the cases that arise in the Federal Courts of each circuit, for the Supreme Court of the United States would be overwhelmed if every such case could be brought before it. There is however a large class of cases where questions of great importance to the public as a whole are decided differently by different Circuit Courts of Appeal. The interpretations of the Sherman Anti-Trust Law vary considerably in different circuits, and cases in which local feeling or prejudice is aroused often go wrong, as has happened where the liability of a city or town to pay its bonds has been questioned. Again, the practice in regard to the appointment of receivers, in theory an interlocutory but in effect often a final decree, has been affected injuriously by the varying action of different judges, and is now in serious confusion. These differences can only be removed by the decision of the Supreme Court, and for that reason and in such cases appeals to that court should be facilitated, and a method provided of promptly determining for example whether a court has erred in taking an individual's property from him, as is now not infrequently done by the appointment *ex parte* of a receiver. Such a decree may ruin a man or a corporation, and the injured party should not be obliged to wait long before it is decided finally whether the decree is right. It is not possible within the limits of these lectures to do more than point out that where the law of the United States must be uniform, the right to invoke the judgment of the Supreme Court should be clearly secured and the process made easy.

The statutes and rules which regulate appeals from one federal court to another are unnecessarily cumbrous and confused. For example, in certain classes of cases it is difficult to decide with all the light that the decisions of the Supreme Court can give, whether an appeal from the Circuit Court should be taken to the Circuit Court of Appeals or to the Supreme Court of the United States, and the choice once made is final. Yet if the litigant chooses wrong the error is fatal. It should be possible with proper care and time to remove such reproaches to our system. The whole federal practice can be much simplified.

## REFORM OF LEGAL PROCEDURE

Assuming that there is to be but one appellate court for almost all cases, what are the delays which attend any appeal, and how can they be avoided?

There are of course the delays which arise in settling the bill of exceptions or other statement of the case on which it is carried up. These arise from the business or laziness of counsel and the indulgence of these by the Court. For them there is no satisfactory remedy except a keener professional conscience on the part of the Bar and less elastic rules or practice on the part of the Bench. The tendency is to extend by legislation the time within which the record for the appeal can be made up, but this should be stoutly combated. There should be a short time fixed by rule, with discretion in the Court to extend it for good reason, and that discretion should be exercised sparingly. My professional experience has satisfied me that when a thing must be done within a certain time it is done, and every postponement makes it harder to do.

## DELAY IN APPELLATE COURTS

It is easier to complete a task which has been begun, than to do it over again from the beginning, and when one returns after an interval to the preparation of an argument or a record, he often finds it necessary to start at the beginning again. The exceptions should be settled while the trial is recent, and its events fresh in the memory.

It is in deciding whether or not to carry a case further that a lawyer needs to remember that he is an officer of the Court, whose duty it is to help in securing justice, and not the willing agent of an angry or unscrupulous client, whose purpose is to delay or defeat it. "It must be presumed," said Mr. Justice Clifford of the Supreme Court of the United States, "that it is the desire of the members of this Bar to have the Court decide right," a violent presumption in some cases perhaps, but which every honorable lawyer should help to justify. He should have the strength and courage to resist his client, and to carry up only substantial questions.

## REFORM OF LEGAL PROCEDURE

The true attitude of a lawyer may perhaps be illustrated by an experience of my own. I advised a client that another man owed him a very large sum of money. Presently the other's counsel appeared in my office, and said, "I hear you have advised A that my client B owes him $100,000." "Yes," said I, "I have." "I suppose," replied he, "that you rely on the case of *Whitcomb* v. *Converse*." "Yes," said I. "I do." "Have you got the report here?" he continued. "If so, let me have it." I handed it to him. "I suppose," he said, "that you rely on this passage in the opinion." I answered that I did. "Don't you see," he went on, "that these words can be read so as to give the passage a different meaning, and that if so read, your advice is wrong?" I looked at the passage again and said, "Perhaps; but I should not be willing to advise my client that such was the true interpretation." "No more should I," he concluded. "It is not. The answer to my suggestion is clear," and he stated it. "I shall advise my client to pay," and he did pay. A weaker man would have carried the question up and lost his case after delaying my client for a year or more, and putting both parties to large expense.

All points are not "free and equal," and a man injures the parties, the reputation of his profession, the administration of justice, and in the long run himself, if he wastes time and money in discussing frivolous points or questions which, however interesting in themselves, do not really affect the merits of his case. In deciding whether to appeal or not, and what questions to raise, as well as in arguing his case, counsel will do well to bear in mind the words of Mr. Justice Hughes, as recently reported in the newspapers. "No lawyer can render a higher service either to his client or to the Court than in the preparation of a complete, candid, intellectual, honest statement and argument of his case to the Court that he addresses. Sophistries, evasions, and the tricks of the pettifogger are indefensible from an

## REFORM OF LEGAL PROCEDURE

ethical standpoint, and are of less avail in winning a case than some imagine."

I cannot too strongly urge upon you all the obligation "to delay no man for lucre or malice," which every lawyer assumes when he enters the Bar. Let me also suggest to you that to present a sophistical argument to the Court is an insult to the intelligence of the Bench. When *you* feel that your contention is unsound, it is safe to assume that this will be at least equally obvious to the trained minds of the judges. No one likes to be taken for a fool, and it is well to remember Hosea Biglow's aphorism: "T'ain't a knowin' kind of cattle that gits ketched with mouldy corn." You will stand better with your judges if you assume that they are as intelligent as yourself, to put it mildly, and also avoid the error of many lawyers who, as one of our Chief Justices said, "present a case on the theory that the Court is thoroughly familiar with the facts, but profoundly ignorant of the law."

## DELAY IN APPELLATE COURTS

And now we stand in the presence of the Court where a critic from the Bar is certainly in a delicate, perhaps in a dangerous position. We have before us three stages — argument, deliberation, and decision, and there is no room for delay by the Bar except in the first stage. Against this the Courts are inclined to set their faces sternly. In England and in some of our states counsel are not limited, but the tendency is strongly the other way. In most of the Federal and State courts the limitation is strict, and extensions are not easy to obtain. As a result counsel are constantly arguing "to the clock instead of to the Court," as one of my friends put it, and in cases where the facts are complicated, and especially where several lawyers are to divide the time allowed, that sense of freedom which a counsel must feel in order to do his case justice is destroyed and he is constantly wondering how far he can go on one point and still have time to develop the others, or how long he can speak without taking time from his associates.

## REFORM OF LEGAL PROCEDURE

Were there no limit set by rule, a court can always convey to counsel the impression that he has talked long enough. I have seen it done by very open indications of weariness, but while these are necessary in extreme cases, they are rarely required. Every competent judge of experience has learned how to indicate without transgressing the laws of courtesy that an argument should not be continued. From the Court's point of view it is not strange that it should wish to protect itself against prolix discussion and foolish argument or indefinite reiteration. The time limit must be retained, but a little more indulgence in important and complicated cases may well be given, especially where the counsel employed are not in the habit of wasting time. The law must be no respecter of persons, but it may well respect methods, and the cause of justice will not suffer if counsel who abuse the indulgence of the Court find it withdrawn, and if on the other hand those who have shown that they deserve the confidence of the Court receive it.

## DELAY IN APPELLATE COURTS

The present practice should make for condensed statement, but it doubtless tends also to increase the length of the printed brief, and perhaps the day is not far distant when all cases may be argued in writing, though against that result should be quoted the remark of Mr. Justice Miller, one of the ablest judges who ever sat on the Supreme Bench of the United States, to Mr. Sidney Bartlett, one of the ablest lawyers who ever appeared before it. "Never submit a case on briefs."

Indeed we could not help regretting the change if oral arguments were abandoned. There is something in the contact between Court and counsel, in the questions of the Court and the answers of the advocate, which stimulates the minds of both, and compels attention while it arouses the necessary interest. Oral argument to the Court is one of the greatest intellectual opportunities which counsel have. and were it given up, much of the romance which attends the practice of the law would be lost. It is true that most of us apprehend more readily with the eye than with the ear, and that we learn the law by reading the reports. But it is also true that one thinks often more effectively on his feet when his brain is full of blood, and can make a better statement or give a more pertinent illustration than occurs to him in the cooler atmosphere of his study. It is also true, that when after a lapse of months one reviews an old brief, he is often surprised to find that it is less cogent and convincing than he thought it when it was written, and that it does not convey to his own mind what he thought it must convey to the mind of the Court. Still if we could be sure as to when and in what circumstances of fatigue, haste, or possible somnolence a brief is read, we might be willing to trust the careful written statement of our case rather than the more or less imperfect presentation possible in a limited oral argument. At present both seem necessary.

One word of practical advice. Never read

## DELAY IN APPELLATE COURTS

your brief to the Court, or read extensive citations from the authorities. The mere repetition of a brief is not an oral argument, only a tedious and useless waste of the Court's time. Unless counsel can state the case clearly and forcibly without reading, unless he can add something to the written brief, his argument does not help the judges, and this part of the law's delay had best be eliminated.

We have now reached the door of the consultation room and here we must pause. We cannot penetrate its secrets. Attempts have been made by statute in some states to insure prompt decisions, but it is impossible to establish a hard and fast rule, or make judges or jurymen agree by the clock.

Mr. Dooley, in one of his inimitable essays, gives voice to an opinion which is too commonly held by the ignorant laity:

"If I had me job to pick out," says he, "I'd be a judge. I've looked over a' the others an' that's th' only wan that suits.

## REFORM OF LEGAL PROCEDURE

I have the judicyal timperament. I hate wurruk."

He traces a capital case through all its stages till it has been argued in the Court of Appeals, and then describes the proceedings as follows:

"Occasionally a judge iv' th' coort iv appeals walkin' in his sleep meets another judge, an' they discuss matthers. 'How arre yer gettin' on with th' Cyanide case, judge?' 'I'm makin' fair headway, judge. I've read part iv th' vardict iv th' coroner's jury las' year, an' nex' month whun th' fishin' is over I expect to look into th' indictment. 'Tis a puzzlin' case. Th' man is not guilty.' 'Well, good-bye, judge. I'll see ye in a year or two. Lave me know how ye're gettin' on. Pleasant dhreams!'" and so they part. . . . "Ye take a lively lawyer that's wurruked twenty hours a day suin' sthreet-railroad companies an' boost him onto a high coort an' he can't think out iv a hammock. Th' more exalted what Hogan calls 'th' joodicial station,' th' more it's like a dormitory."

DELAY IN APPELLATE COURTS

This is all very amusing, and as untrue in its essence as it is funny, but there is a vein of truth in it as there is in every one of Mr. Dooley's essays. The late Judge John Lowell of the Circuit Court said that he made it a rule to decide cases in the order in which they were argued, and this may be commended as a salutary practice. The moment that a judge or anyone else falls into the habit of dealing with the easy cases first, he is apt to postpone the hard ones, salving his conscience with the feeling that he is diligently at work and cannot be blamed for deferring a very difficult case till he has more leisure, rather than delay perhaps more persons by keeping them waiting while he ploughs through a long record and decides very close questions of fact or law. I am old enough to know however that the longer such things are postponed, the more they grow to resemble mountains, and the harder it is to take them up at any given time. Mr. Dooley helps us in this matter when he describes all that he finds to do in a morning when he has a serious job to tackle, how he reads the newspaper backward and forward, advertisements and all, and how he catches at every excuse for postponing the hard work that awaits him. There are no harder worked or more conscientious men than the judges of our appellate courts, but they are men, and Judge Lowell's rule would often help them. The very fact that an important and difficult case was a dam behind which a multitude of cases was accumulating would exercise a pressure, and by giving one's whole time to a case much can be accomplished. Anthony Trollope made it a rule to write a certain number of words every day, and he accomplished it by sitting down at a given hour and going at once to work. A pen in one's hand is a great help to progress, and the late Judge Hoar used to say that he considered his opinion half written when he took a sheet of paper and wrote at the top "Hoar J." It is the beginning that is hard, and the feeling that work is to be done tires most of us more than doing it.

## DELAY IN APPELLATE COURTS

If these words of mine can be tortured into a suggestion to our judges, it is made with the greatest respect, and with a full appreciation of the difficulties which surround them.

Delays in the lower courts are much less excusable, for it is often more important to have a decision than what the decision is. If wrong, a higher court can correct the error, but if no decision at all is made, the injury is irreparable. It would be better to have a judge decide many cases on his impressions at the close of the argument than hold his decision, as I have known a motion for a new trial to be held, for four years. It is fatally easy to put a band round the papers and lay them away for a leisure time in the indefinite future. For this delay it is not easy to suggest any remedy, except such as is found in the election of strong men for judicial positions, and the creation of a public sentiment among the members of the Bar which shall support them in the fearless discharge of their duties.

REFORM OF LEGAL PROCEDURE

With all due respect, however, I may be permitted to suggest that the time occupied by any appellate tribunal in reading its judgments, often extended by reading several concurring or dissenting opinions, is a pure waste of time. As no one knows in advance when the decision in a given case will be announced, the parties and their counsel are rarely present, and the opinions are often read to an audience entirely without interest in the case decided. It is difficult to see what useful purpose is served by a practice which in most appellate courts has been abandoned, but which is still adhered to in the highest of all.

So much for the delay which besets the course of legal proceedings from the commencement of suit till its final determination by the court of last resort. But its judgment is often not final. Some error of law or procedure is held to vitiate all that has been done, and the litigant is compelled to begin again. Such results are inevitable, but they are also deplorable, and a reversal for anything that does not go to the merits of the cause is especially unfortunate. The American Bar Association has suggested one remedy for this difficulty, and has urged Congress to pass a statute which contains the following provisions:

"No judgment shall be set aside, or reversed, or new trial granted, by any court of the United States in any case, civil or criminal, on the ground of misdirection of the jury or the improper admission or rejection of evidence, or for error as to any matter of pleading or procedure, unless, in the opinion of the court to which application is made, after an examination of the entire cause, it shall appear that the error complained of has injuriously affected the substantial rights of the parties."

This statute applies only to the Federal Courts, but each state can make a similar law for its own courts, or in the absence of statute courts may properly decide that errors are immaterial and therefore not ground for reversal. It is the true rule, and should be applied inflexibly in aid of the principle, "*Interest rei publicae ut sit finis litium.*" If the decision below is just it should be sustained, and not reversed in order that immaterial errors may be corrected with the risk that in a new trial other like errors, perhaps material, may be committed, and the whole subject of the litigation be consumed by the expense of determining not the rights of the parties, but the ideally perfect method of conducting a trial. Such a statute will not only prevent many needless new trials, but it will discourage appeals on technical grounds, it will reduce the expense of litigation to clients and the expense of maintaining courts to the public, it will reduce the congestion in the courts which is a constant cause of delay, and it will increase the confidence of the public in the administration of justice.

But it may be said: "Can we trust the appellate courts to decide whether an error has or has not injuriously affected the substantial rights of the parties," in other words, "Can we trust our highest courts to decide what is right in a given case?" We must trust some one to decide this question, and if we cannot trust the highest Court, whom can we trust? Everything human is fallible, and no system can exclude the possibility of error, but that measure of practical justice which is all that any human being can expect in a mortal world is amply secured by such a rule as the proposed statute prescribes, and it is infinitely less likely to result in a denial of justice than the present practice. It is a rule which demands good judges, but these are always essential if justice is to be done under any system.

You must have observed that for many of the troubles which I have pointed out my remedy has been increased power in the judges, and this of course can only be given to an able, strong, independent Bench. How important is this, and how is it to be secured? The people of the United States plume themselves on their sound practical common sense, but there is no single matter in which they have so long and so persistently displayed a lack of this quality as in dealing with their judges. Our whole political structure rests upon the assumption that the judiciary shall have power to hold the balance between the different departments of the government, shall protect the legislature against usurpation by the executive, shall defend the executive against encroachment by the legislature, shall maintain the right of every citizen against invasion by any other, and shall shield a minority of perhaps only one against oppression by the majority, however large. It must hold the scales of justice even between government and citizen, between strong and weak. Yet to use the words of Hamilton:

"From the nature of its functions it will always be the least dangerous to the political rights of the Constitution because it will be least in a capacity to annoy or injure them. The executive not only dispenses the honors, but holds the sword of the community; the legislature not only commands the purse but prescribes the rules by which the duties and rights of every citizen are to be regulated; the judiciary on the contrary has no influence over either the sword or the purse, no direction of either the strength, or of the wealth of the society, and can take no active resolution whatever. It may truly be said to have neither force nor will, but merely judgment, and must ultimately depend upon the aid of the executive arm for the efficacious exercise even of this faculty."

A body of men upon whom such great responsibilities are laid, and who can accomplish the results expected of them only by the effect which is produced upon the public mind by the excellence of their judgments; who can only declare what is just and in the long run must depend upon the conviction which their declaration carries for its influence, should be composed of the ablest and wisest men that the country can supply. There is nothing which is so important to the state as a strong and independent Bench, there is nothing which costs so much as cheap courts, nothing so dear as injustice.

The Courts sit to maintain and enforce the law, — which is the well-considered will of the State and the State needs and can afford the best talent to support its will. The large organizations, the great corporations, the men of wealth, the most dangerous criminals, command the services of the ablest lawyers. The courts should stand between any unjust claims of such persons and the community. The judges should be able enough to recognize sophistry and see through improper appeals, they should be learned enough to know what the law requires in each case, they should be strong enough to meet great advocates on equal terms, and to protect poorer clients and weaker lawyers against injustice. Strength, ability, knowledge, and character are essential to a good judge, and where they are lacking we have error, tediously protracted proceedings, frequent new trials, delay, and expense both to suitors and the community.

## DELAY IN APPELLATE COURTS

Where weak courts deal with criminals, crime goes unpunished, lawlessness flourishes, men lose their respect for the courts and resort to lynch law, and civilization suffers. It is impossible to overestimate the loss which bad courts inflict on a community, and there is no better test of a people's position in the scale of civilization than the character of its judicial tribunals, as will become apparent to you if you will compare the methods by which justice is administered in different nations.

But how are good judges to be obtained? The public needs as good lawyers as any private interest, and can afford as well to pay what is needed to obtain them, but it cannot afford not to have them or to be content with poor service. The state comes into the market as a customer, and finds itself in competition with other purchasers. If it needs land it must pay the market price, if it needs food or clothes for its soldiers it must pay what others pay for like quantities of the same things. The same inexorable law of supply and demand applies when it seeks the service of men. It must pay an adequate price or it will not succeed in the competition with those who offer more. The price is not necessarily all to be paid in money. There are many men who are attracted to public office by the honor attached to it or by the prospect of assured employment, and there are others who are influenced by a sense of public duty and are willing to make some patriotic sacrifice, but an adequate salary is in the long run essential. Lawyers are men, they have wives and children and wish to give them the advantages of travel and the pleasures of society. A judge has a position to maintain, and the lawyer who is well established in practice and happy in his home and his prospects is loath to take the vow of poverty, to deny his children what their companions enjoy, to accept a position which carries him sometimes for long periods away from home to live in a poor hotel while he is holding a term, to find himself cut off from the pleasant society to which he is accustomed and to a certain extent isolated by his position and the necessity of guarding against unjust suspicions; in a word, to give up a free, interesting, busy, prosperous life for one in which he is restricted on every side. This is less true of the higher than the lower judicial positions, for the honor of the former is so great that men are willing to sacrifice something to win them, but even here the choice is restricted by the considerations which I have pointed out. A judgeship should be with us, as it always has been in England, among the prizes of the profession which a leader is glad to accept as the crown of a successful career. Under present conditions it is a place which a man of independent means, or a man whose professional success has been limited may wish to take, but which cannot be taken by a successful lawyer without a sacrifice. I speak from recent experience in endeavoring as one of a committee to find men, who were fit to fill and willing to accept a seat on the Bench. Man after man whom we thought fit refused, because he felt that he must save for wife and children, and he could not do this on the Bench and live comfortably without changing his methods. Others disliked to give up their freedom, and only a few felt able, or willing from a sense of duty to make the sacrifice which everyone felt that he must make in accepting the appointment.

This was where the judges are appointed for life. Where they are elected by the people for shorter or longer terms, the difficulty of securing good judges is enormously increased. In the first place the people at large cannot judge as to certain elements of fitness, as, for example, the candidate's knowledge of the law. If a man is a candidate for re-election his service during his previous term or terms may be a guide, but not so when he is originally selected. Many qualities make a man popular with the voters which unfit him for the Bench, and the chance of a wise selection is small, especially in communities

## DELAY IN APPELLATE COURTS

where men of different races and perhaps different religions are more anxious to have these represented on the Bench than to secure the best possible judges.

Again we find that in New York, for example, a candidate is expected to contribute a year's salary or a considerable part of it, to the campaign fund of the party which supports him. There must be many men who would make admirable judges, but who would absolutely refuse to buy a nomination or election in this way, and many others who will not expose themselves to the disagreeable attacks that are made during a campaign upon all candidates. The best men will not seek judicial office on such terms. To enter a political contest for nomination or election, and especially to pay for judicial office, is an impossibility for many men, and under the elective system men of this class become ineligible.

Again, the judge whose election is approaching and who dreads defeat must find it very difficult, indeed often impossible, to decide against a

## REFORM OF LEGAL PROCEDURE

popular litigant or a lawyer influential in politics, or to set aside a law which the people approve. Human nature is weak, and a good judge must be strong enough to stand by his own convictions of justice and law against any and all attacks, whether from counsel in court or public opinion without. We need judges who love justice more than they love their offices, and we do wrong when we expose them to temptations which human nature finds it hard to resist. When, as now, it is proposed that the people may recall them before their term expires, it is inevitable that with the axe suspended over their judicial necks they should find it much harder to decide right, — much easier to swim with the popular current. The umpire at a baseball match has at least one side to support his decision, but the judge who holds a popular law unconstitutional or makes some other unpopular decision may well have no friends. The Massachusetts Bill of Rights states the true rule in these words:

## DELAY IN APPELLATE COURTS

"It is essential to the preservation of the rights of every individual, his life, liberty, property, and character, that there be an impartial interpretation of the laws and administration of justice. It is the right of every citizen to be tried by judges as free, impartial, and independent as the lot of humanity will admit. It is therefore not only the best policy, but for the security of the rights of the people and of every citizen, that the judges of the Supreme Judicial Court should hold their offices as long as they behave themselves well, and that they should have honorable salaries, ascertained and established by existing laws."

We make the entrance to the Bench difficult by compelling the candidate too often to seek and pay for election at the hands of the people. We make his tenure uncertain. We show that we do not trust him by limiting his powers in every way, and we pay him a grossly inadequate salary. We are a business people; we know that in private life we could not get a good foreman on these terms, and we wonder that our courts are choked and the administration of the law expensive and uncertain. *What common sense!*

A Kentucky judge said to the Bar Association of that state last year:

"Our jealousy of the judge is such that we have formulated a set of hard and fast rules for his guidance — absolute rules of evidence, strict reviews of every act, word, or ruling by the Court of Appeals. We have devised special machinery to eliminate the personality of the judge. At the same time we have given increased rein to the advocate as well as to the shyster, till now the judge must daily 'sit like a knot in a log' and listen to speeches to the jury — speeches that are the disgrace of our civilization — and daily watch practices which he is powerless to prevent and which are recognized by all the community as void of all semblance of morality. To make matters worse, we have made our judges — all of them — mere puppets of political

## DELAY IN APPELLATE COURTS

parties, so that it is impossible for them or any of them to be independent as I know everyone of our judges would wish to be."

Such a picture does not make the Bench attractive.

Think for a moment that we spend out of a billion dollars appropriated for the annual expenses of the nation seventy-two per cent. for war, past and future, and then compare this with the beggarly sum allowed for the expenses of the Federal Courts. Millions of dollars for force that we hope never to use, and a few thousands for justice that we need every day of our lives! I hardly know which costs us most, the expensive battleships or the cheap courts. If we doubled the salary of every judge on the Bench the cost would be trifling as compared with the cost of a Dreadnought, yet the dangers to which poor courts expose us are far greater and more imminent than any from which our fleet protects us. Yet we boast of our common sense.

## REFORM OF LEGAL PROCEDURE

We have been far more fortunate than we deserve in securing excellent judges, and what I say is not intended to reflect in any way upon their ability or their character, but to point out that we do not treat them fairly. Our system is wrong, and we cannot long expect that it will yield good results. Nay, it is certain that it will yield steadily worse results if it is continued.

The full argument against an elective judiciary has been presented so often that I will not repeat it, nor have I time to say more than I have on the subject. The difference between a proper method of securing judges and the method which we employ is shown by a single fact. In England the ablest, strongest, and most experienced lawyers are placed on the Bench, and the result is that English justice is proverbial. In many parts of our country young men with little experience obtain judgeships as a step towards practice, intending to resign and commence practice with the prestige which is conferred by the much abused title "judge." In England the fittest, and in the communities of which I speak perhaps the unfittest, administer justice. "By their fruits ye shall know them."

The profession must combine to uphold the power and dignity of the Bench, and to make judicial positions attractive to the ablest lawyers in every jurisdiction. Unless this is done, the grave defects in our system will remain unchanged.

I have discussed with you now the causes of delay and have suggested some remedies. Let me now deal with something which is not a remedy. It is constantly urged that in order to overcome the delay in the courts we should have more judges and so more courts. My remedy is better courts with greater powers. The usual remedy is more courts with less powers. Let me call your attention to some figures taken for convenience from my own state, but which illustrate conditions in many states. In 1874, we had in Massachusetts ten judges of the Superior Court. We have now twenty-five. The population has not quite doubled. If we compare

## REFORM OF LEGAL PROCEDURE

Massachusetts with England, we find that in 1900 Massachusetts had a population of 2,800,000 people; that in 1901 England had a population of 32,527,000, between 11 and 12 times as great. In the higher courts of England there are 34 judges. In the higher courts of Massachusetts there are 51 judges. If we take the County Courts in England and the corresponding courts in Massachusetts we find that England has in all 93 judges, and Massachusetts has 144 judges. Dealing only with the higher courts, England has a judge to each 956,700 people; Massachusetts has a judge for every 56,968. If we take all the judges, England has a judge for each 349,762, Massachusetts a judge for each 19,520 persons. To put it in another way, if England adopted the Massachusetts ratio, and had as many judges as there are in Massachusetts, England would have 570 higher court judges, instead of 34, nearly twenty times as many, and she would have 1666 judges in all instead of 93. This comparison is to a very slight extent misleading,

## DELAY IN APPELLATE COURTS

because whenever you have a separate judicial system, you must have appellate courts of several judges no matter what the population. But the English Appellate Court sits with fewer judges than the Supreme Court of Massachusetts.

Some years ago I was told that there were fewer juries sitting in London than in Boston. There were, as I remember it, in October three special juries and three ordinary juries, in all six, sitting in London with its enormous population. We had in Boston some eight or ten juries sitting at the same time, counting the juries in the Federal courts. If you go into our trial courts, you find on the trial list for the day an enormous number of cases. If you go into an English court, you find three, but those three are to be tried on that day, and, as a rule, they are tried. Yet, with this smaller force, fewer juries and fewer judges, they do the work of 32,000,000 of people, which shows that the character and not the number of the courts is the essential factor.

In Chicago a judge disposes of nearly 1000

REFORM OF LEGAL PROCEDURE

cases a year; in England each judge disposes of more than 3500 cases a year, yet English justice is satisfactory. In 1902, out of more than 46,000 cases disposed of by the county courts, there were only 140 appeals. Out of 689 cases heard on appeal in 1902, 106 were disposed of in two weeks after the hearing; 101 in four weeks. The average delay was less than six months. Many were decided on the spot. Out of 555 cases which were heard on appeal in 1904, the judgment was reserved in only 50.

In Montana, with its 240,000 people, the Supreme Court was lately two years in arrears. In England 550 cases were heard on appeal in 1904, and of these 500 were decided before the counsel left the court room. It is clear that we do not need more judges, and it is worth while to remember, when this remedy is suggested, that more judges do not mean less delay. As in other things quality not quantity tells.

It is also worth while to bear in mind that increasing the number of judges of the Appellate

## DELAY IN APPELLATE COURTS

Court does not always conduce to better results. It takes longer for seven or nine men to agree on a proposition of law than it does for three, and in reaching the result, each takes less responsibility than if he was one of three. The larger the tribunal, the longer time it takes to reach a decision, the greater the chance of disagreement without improving the result. We do not want more men upon the Bench. We want a better system, and we want the best men.

It is also suggested that unanimity should no longer be required from a jury, and that a majority should be allowed to render the verdict. This suggestion is founded on an exaggerated impression as to the frequency of disagreements. In the year ending June 30, 1909, out of 893 cases tried in Boston the jury agreed in all but 31, of which 30 were in tort cases. Unanimity insures consideration. It compels the jury to listen and gives the wisest man a chance to make himself heard which he might not otherwise have. It also gives an obstinate fool an equal chance, and if disagreements were frequent the change might be necessary. As it is, the advantages secured by the requirement outweigh the disadvantages. There may be a few less verdicts, but as a whole the verdicts are better. Very little of the law's delay is chargeable to jurymen, who agree oftener than the judges of appellate courts.

# V

## CRIMINAL PROCEDURE. THE LAWYER'S RESPONSIBILITIES FOR LEGISLATION

THERE is no part of its work in which the law fails so absolutely and so ludicrously as in the conviction and punishment of criminals, and its failures in this respect endanger the whole foundation of society. As our population increases and becomes more varied in character crime appears to increase, and it becomes more difficult to discover criminals of the lower type. An embezzler who has moved in high financial circles, or an identified murderer like Dr. Crippen, will indeed find it more difficult to escape, but where a crime is committed by some person unknown, where the motive is robbery and there is no antecedent relation between the criminal and his victim, detection is very difficult. Burglars and villains

of like kinds are no longer restrained by national boundaries. The men who robbed a jeweller's shop in Boston some years ago were found last week in an Austrian prison. Misgovernment in Russia supplied the criminals who some years ago robbed and murdered a cashier in a crowded London neighborhood, and a year ago men of the same nationality committed the identical crime in Massachusetts. The complicity of the police with criminals of certain classes in at least some of our large cities, the difficulty of proving certain crimes like bribery, the weak sentimentality of the community, which, when a horrible crime is committed, shrieks for the detection and punishment of the perpetrator, and when he is found seeks to find excuses for his act and reasons for his pardon, all weaken the restraints which the law is intended to impose upon the depraved members of society. To all these difficulties our courts, by their administration of the law, and our whole system of criminal procedure add as many more.

## LAWYER'S RESPONSIBILITIES

The figures are startling. Judge Holt of New York, in an address last June, estimated that there were 100,000 men who had taken part in lynchings, and over 150,000 who had participated in strike riots resulting in homicide and injury to persons and property, who had gone unpunished. The Chicago "Tribune" gives figures which show that from 1887 to 1908, inclusive, the number of homicides committed in the United States increased from 1266 to nearly 9000. In fifteen years the total number was 133,192, while during the four years of our Civil War the whole number of men on the Union side who were killed or died of their wounds was 110,070. In Louisville, Kentucky, during the year ending August 1st last, forty-seven homicides were committed and there was not one legal execution, while during the year 1909 in the city of London with its enormous population there were only nineteen cases of murder. Of these murderers five committed suicide, four were convicted and executed, four were found to be insane, one died while waiting trial, and one killed himself in jail.

President Andrew D. White says that in our whole country during the same year there were only seventy convictions in capital cases, and lays this result "to the chicanery, pettifoggery, and folly in the defence of criminals." "The murder rate in the United States is from ten to twenty times greater than the murder rate of the British Empire and other northwestern European countries."

The New Bedford "Standard" quotes Dr. White's statement and adds:

"Dr. White speaks none too strongly. That attitude toward crime which makes of the criminal nothing more than an "unfortunate" is responsible for very much of the criminality of to-day. Under its influence a young tough who sets fire to a dwelling house is now enumerated as a "delinquent," a word selected for fear that any harsher term would hurt his feelings. When he gets a little older, and repeats his act of arson, immediately uprises a phalanx of the soft-hearted to proclaim him "a victim of society's neglect," and he very likely escapes any serious punishment because the prosecuting officer is willing to accept an alienist's assurance that he is a "pyro-maniac." If anybody suggests at any stage of his career that he has some responsibility of his own, a chorus of strident voices joins in the chant that our weaker brethren should be the object of our considerate pity."

The object of criminal law is the detection and punishment of crime, and its strict enforcement is necessary, not only to protect the community against the criminals, but also against itself. When a crime is committed the feeling that somebody should be punished is instantly felt by all within the neighborhood affected. It is a feeling compounded of revenge, fear, and a sense of justice, and is most intense at the first news of the crime. If the neighborhood feels that the law will punish surely and promptly, it will let the law take its course. If it feels that the law will let the guilty man escape, it is prone to take the law into its own hands, and punish the person whom it suspects, with or without sufficient evidence of his guilt.

The contrast between the feeling of the community outside and the attitude of juries within the courts is thus stated in the Chicago "Advance":

"But the general public cannot be persuaded that making murder easy is good for a community. During the editor's recent visit to the South he was surprised to find how much the public is disturbed by the failure to punish murderers. In Birmingham it was said that murderers slipped through the courts with ease. A jury had just cleared a man for killing the proprietor of the hotel at which the editor stopped. It seemed a wanton crime, but the jury took an easy view of the matter. In Florida there was similar feeling. Men killed their fellow-men, and between juries, shrewd lawyers, and the law's loopholes and delays, they were out in the open

## LAWYER'S RESPONSIBILITIES

again as if nothing much had happened. About the only line drawn with firmness was on color. On the same day that it was made so trifling a matter in Nashville for a colonel to assassinate a former United States senator, the citizens of Meridian, Miss., lynched, shot, hanged, and burnt a negro for killing a white man. When a negro kills a man it is a fiendish crime, but when a colonel kills a distinguished citizen it is an affair between gentlemen, and, according to the Tennessee governor's view of the matter, it is a piece of impudence for the courts, lower or higher, to try to make it embarrassing to the chief actor in the tragedy."

Well does President Eliot say:

"The defenses of society against criminals have broken down. The impunity with which crimes of violence are committed is a disgrace to the country."

The inevitable result is lynch law with all its disastrous effects on society, the killing of innocent persons without trial, the inhuman methods often employed, the brutalizing effect on perpetrators and spectators, and the destruction of all real respect for the law which is the foundation of civilized society. All these consequences flow directly from the lax administration of criminal law, and where courts cannot protect the innocent and punish the guilty, private war and social disorganization are near.

This is not an exaggerated picture. You have only to think of the brutal lynchings in the South and North, of the night riders in Kentucky where neighbor killed neighbor, where men burned each others' houses, and visited on each other every kind of outrage because they differed as to the terms upon which, or the customers to which, they should sell their tobacco; the labor war in Colorado, and like illustrations in different parts of the country to see that I speak well within bounds. "Sooner or later," as a Southern writer says, "the community which tolerates mob law will feel the violence of some new form of lawlessness."

## LAWYER'S RESPONSIBILITIES

There is no real civilization, and as Secretary Dickinson said: "There can be no general and steady economic development where there is a general non-enforcement of law," and the inevitable result may be gathered from this statement made three days after the Atlanta riot in 1906 by Charles T. Hopkins, a member of the Chamber of Commerce, and a prominent Atlanta business man:

"Saturday evening at eight o'clock, the credit of Atlanta was good for any number of millions of dollars in New York or Boston, or any financial center; to-day we couldn't borrow fifty cents. The reputation we have been building up so arduously for years has been swept away in two short hours, not by men who have made and make Atlanta, not by men who represent the character and strength of our city, but by hoodlums, understrappers, and white criminals."

Yet how completely the community accepts lawless methods, unconscious of the danger, may be gathered from the following:

## REFORM OF LEGAL PROCEDURE

A certain newspaper correspondent ventured to describe a recent Mississippi mob as composed of ruffians. Whereupon Tax Assessor Miller of Concordia Parish, La., which is just across the river from the scene of the lynching, sharply rebuked him in the following marvelous letter:

"The lynching of Elmo Curl at Mastodon, Miss., last night, was a most orderly affair, conducted by the bankers, lawyers, farmers, and merchants of that county. The best people of the county, as good as there are anywhere, simply met there and hanged Curl without a sign of rowdyism. There was no drinking, no shooting, no yelling, and not even any loud talking. All of the best people of that section took part, and I have never seen a more orderly assemblage anywhere."

To accomplish its purpose, criminal procedure should be simple, prompt, and effectual. The guilty should feel that the arm of the law is sure and strong. To-day the law as administered throws around the criminal a protecting wall

## LAWYER'S RESPONSIBILITIES

which may have been necessary when the power of the English crown pressed despotically upon the subject, but which is wholly unnecessary to-day. It is the community that now needs protection against the criminal, not the innocent man who must be saved from unjust persecution. To-day it is said with a certain bitter truth that the only man whose life is safe is he who has been convicted of murder.

What are the difficulties? The detection and arrest of the criminal are for the police, and with the difficulties which beset these the courts have little to do. We will assume that the accused has been caught and the evidence laid before the grand jury. Their first step is to find an indictment, and to this the defendant is required to plead.

Now the whole object of an indictment is to inform the court, the jury, and the prisoner of what the charge against the prisoner is. As a rule no one knows so well as the accused exactly what he has done, and what the indictment means. There is no reason why the indictment should not state the charge in the simplest and most direct language, as for example, why an indictment for murder should not be in as few words as the following:

"The grand jurors charge that A. on the 1st day of March at Boston in the County of Suffolk did commit murder by killing B."

A form substantially like this is now used in England and her colonies, and there is no crime which cannot be charged with equal brevity. Such an indictment informs the accused of exactly the charge against him, and accomplishes every purpose of an indictment. If it is insufficient and he wants further information in any case, he can be given the right to move for specifications, and in a proper case the Court would grant them, or the prosecution should be allowed to amend, but whenever the jury is impanelled all questions as to the nature of the charge should be regarded as finally settled.

Under the practice which now prevails almost

everywhere in this country, the indictment is used as a trap for the prosecution and a bulwark for the defence. The ingenuity of the State's attorney is taxed to the utmost in the effort to be sure that his indictment complies with every technicality, while the defendant's counsel exerts every faculty to find a flaw in his opponent's statement, so that instead of trying the guilt or innocence of the prisoner, the trial too frequently is reduced to a question as to the necessity of a few absurd words in an indictment. The so-called "flaw in the indictment" is uniformly the resort of a convicted criminal. If the trial ends in an acquittal, either by order of the Court or verdict of the jury, the prosecution cannot appeal, since the defendant cannot twice be placed in jeopardy. It is only after a trial in which all the evidence has been sifted, and the question of guilt or innocence thoroughly argued, a trial in which the defendant has known exactly what he was charged with, and where the verdict has been so clearly right that either the defendant's counsel has not asked the trial court to set it aside, or the motion has been made and denied, that the Appellate Court is asked to reverse the judgment, not because the defendant is not guilty, and not because he has not been fairly tried, but because an indictment sufficient to inform everybody of the charge has or has not contained a few idle words. Too often, though no one has been prejudiced by the omission, the Court lets the guilty rascal go, not because justice requires it, but for no better reason than to preserve a particular fashion of speech.

Do you want examples? Let me give you some from American courts within a few years. One man was convicted of murder in the first degree, and the verdict was set aside because the foreman spelled "first" "fust." In another case a convicted murderer was given a new trial because "breast" was spelled in the indictment without the "a." Another murderer was given a new trial, because, though the indictment alleged that he stabbed a man who did "instantly die," the words "then and there" were not inserted before "instantly," as if he could have died instantly without dying "then and there," or as if it made any difference when or where he died if he was killed by the accused. Again, an indictment for rape was held defective because it concluded "against peace and dignity of the State" instead of "against *the* peace and dignity of the State," and a conviction of murder was set aside because in the name of the murdered man, Patrick Fitz-Patrick, the second "patrick" was spelled with a small "p."

Verdicts have been set aside because the record did not show that the defendant pleaded not guilty, and again because it did not show that he was present at the trial. In the first case he either pleaded guilty, not guilty, or *nolo contendere*, or else stood silent, in which case the Court would have entered a plea of "not guilty," and he had been tried and convicted, so that whatever his plea, it had become of no possible conse-

## REFORM OF LEGAL PROCEDURE

quence. In the second, if he had not been present at the trial his counsel might have been trusted to make the point, and the record would have shown his absence. In both cases a slight respect for the rule *"Omnia praesumuntur rite acta"* would have saved the profession the mortification of admitting that we have courts capable of making such absurd decisions in favor of convicted murderers.

I cannot refrain from giving one more instance of fatuity where an indictment charged that B. killed D. "by firing a Colt's revolver loaded with gunpowder and leaden balls, which he, B., then and there had and held in his hands." The defendant was convicted, but the Court set the conviction aside because the indictment did not allege that the pistol was fired at D. "It may have been fired into the air, or at a flock of birds. Nor can we see that D. was hit; he may have been a feeble man who died of fright at the discharge of the pistol for anything the indictment contains!" If either of these things had

## LAWYER'S RESPONSIBILITIES

been true, of course the defendant would never have been convicted, and "the law is the perfection of human reason." Can you wonder that it falls into disrepute when it is so interpreted?

How often do the most important prosecutions fail from such absurdities. A flaw in the indictment set free the convicted mayor of Minneapolis after a full and fair trial. Similar defences proved fatal to most of the important convictions won by Governor Folk at St. Louis, when men who had betrayed their fellow citizens by selling franchises and contracts, bribers and bribed alike, were relieved from the consequences of their crimes by the highest court of Missouri. One of the most conspicuous among these rascals said, after he had been sentenced to a term in the penitentiary: "The Courts will reverse all Folk's cases, and when Folk's term expires we will get off and the fellows that have peached will go to jail!" He knew whereof he spoke. How long has it taken in San Francisco to get Abe Ruef, a conspicuous rascal who had pleaded guilty, into the prison cell which he should long ago have occupied? And when in the light of plain common sense one asks why these decisions are made, it is impossible to imagine a reason at once honest and sensible. It we cannot alter the law so as to make such mockeries of justice impossible, our profession deserves the contempt of the community. One remedy for this difficulty is to be found in statutes prescribing simple forms of indictment, and giving the Court power to afford the defendant such information as is necessary to relieve any doubts as to the crime charged, if such doubt exists.

Let us take another step, and assuming that the indictment is correct, proceed to the trial. In the first place a jury must be impanelled, and the Court too often finds the simple task of selecting twelve impartial men almost beyond its powers. In New York, when Thaw was tried, in Tennessee when the murderers of Senator Carmack were set at the bar, weeks elapsed in trying jurymen. Ninety-one days

## LAWYER'S RESPONSIBILITIES

were consumed in the selection of a jury to try Calhoun in San Francisco. To get a jury who should try one Shea, 9425 jurymen were summoned, of whom 4821 were examined, the cost in jury fees alone being more than $13,000. In England and in most New England states this difficulty does not arise, and the impanelling of a jury is accomplished easily. At the trial of Dr. Crippen the jury was selected in eight minutes, and only three jurors were challenged, yet the Crippen case, the evidence, the flight and capture of the accused had occupied columns in every daily newspaper for weeks. One English judge stated that in fourteen years he had known only one challenge.

Where a defendant is allowed to challenge anyone who has got an impression from reading the newspaper and has moreover many peremptory challenges, the process is a travesty of justice. This is a country where the newspapers live largely by printing full narratives of crime with every suggestion bearing on the guilt or innocence of each suspected person, that the ingenuity of a reporter or editor can supply. Day after day, suspicions, theories, and arguments are spread before the public, and as in most communities it would be very difficult to find an intelligent man who does not read some newspaper, it is naturally difficult to find a juryman who has not some impression. We all read such accounts more or less carelessly, but our opinions, if any, are not lasting, and are easily corrected by evidence. The counsel who wishes to keep an intelligent man off the jury, the juror who is glad to be excused from the disagreeable task of trying a man for his life or for some other felony, unite to magnify the reasons for not serving, and man after man who could sit with perfect propriety and render a just verdict is excused from service. The result cannot fail to be a poor jury and generally an unsatisfactory result. Why should we continue to countenance a system, which aims to get a weak jury, and make the enforcement of the law more

## LAWYER'S RESPONSIBILITIES

difficult. Peremptory challenges should be few, and judges should keep any man on the jury who is otherwise qualified and who has not a decided opinion as to the guilt or innocence of the accused. We should use some of our boasted common sense, and no longer tolerate the absurdities which make our criminal trials so often mere mockeries.

Something might also be said in favor of preventing the press from trying all suspected persons in their columns, as is now done. It is a flagrant abuse and a great impediment to justice. The newspapers might well be forbidden to publish anything concerning a case that is actually in court, except accurate reports of proceedings in court. After the Crippen case was tried, the publisher of a newspaper was heavily fined for publishing a false statement that Crippen had confessed, and if this precedent were followed here the newspaper statements which now embarrass the course of justice might be less common.

## REFORM OF LEGAL PROCEDURE

Let us now suppose that the jury has been impanelled, and proceed with the trial. Here again we find every precaution taken to protect the guilty.

In the first place the Constitution provides that "no person shall be compelled in any criminal case to be a witness against himself." Originally the criminal could not testify at all, but statutes have given him this right, and have coupled it with the provision that if he elects not to take the stand no argument shall be made or inference drawn against him on account of his refusal.

The practical absurdity of this provision is illustrated by the charge given by a very able judge in Massachusetts, who was asked to instruct the jury that no inference could be drawn from the fact that the defendant did not take the stand.

"Yes," he said, "gentlemen, that's the law and we're all bound to obey the law. If the legislature were to pass a law that when you walk down State Street and see the shadow of the old State House thrown across the street, you are not to infer that the sun is shining, you'd be bound to obey it, gentlemen, and so you're bound to obey this law!"

Another judge of our state said with much truth, "When the common law undertook to find a fact it began by excluding from the room all the persons who would be likely to have any knowledge of the subject," to wit, the parties to the suit and all persons interested in the question to be tried. The rule which I am discussing is a conspicuous example of this absurd principle. The accused of all men in the world knows better than any one else whether he is guilty or not, and if the object of the criminal law is to detect and punish the guilty, why should he not be asked to tell what he knows? If he criminates himself, can there be better evidence of guilt? Why shouldn't he criminate himself? Eye-witnesses may be mistaken, circumstantial evidence may mislead, but the testimony of the accused against himself can be relied upon in any but the most exceptional cases. One can imagine circumstances in which the accused may say what he does not mean, or may criminate himself unjustly. True, and we can cite cases of mistaken identity, cases where innocent men have been convicted upon circumstantial evidence, nay even cases where the defendant's own confessions have proved false, but we do not on that account exclude the evidence of eyewitnesses, the admissions of the accused, or circumstantial evidence. Nothing human is perfect, no testimony is infallible, but of all evidence which tends to establish the defendant's guilt, his own is least likely to be unreliable. He may, and in most cases does lie to save himself, but never if he knows it to accuse himself.

The rule in question, originally adopted to save the subject from the tyrannical power of the Crown when men were persecuted for religious opinions, for political offences, for writing or speaking the truth, is preserved, though the reason for it has long disappeared. The danger now is, not that innocent men will be convicted, but that guilty men will go unwhipped of justice. Not only do the Courts protect the criminal, but the community watches the trial with jealous eyes, and if the murderer or other criminal is convicted, no matter how justly, the newspapers are filled with misrepresentations of the evidence and with appeals to sympathy! Petitions for pardon are circulated and generally signed, some sensational newspaper takes up the convict's cause and attacks the Court which convicted him, until, as Mr. Dooley puts it: "th' insurance comp'nies insure his life for the lowest known premyum." While this is the attitude of the community, there is no danger that what it is now the fashion to call "a gruelling cross-examination," or a brow-beating judge, will confuse an innocent man and make him admit guilt. Any such methods would surely raise popular sympathy and the offender would be visited with public reprobation. These bugbears need not disturb us. It is the community

## REFORM OF LEGAL PROCEDURE

and not the criminal that now needs protection, and if the community is to be protected it can only be by the prompt and sure administration of justice. It is the certainty rather than the severity of punishment that is needed to repress crime.

In France and Germany, for many years, the practice of having the accused interrogated in the presence of the jury by the judge who presides at his trial has been pursued, and while occasional scenes occur which impress us who are accustomed to English methods as unpleasant, it is always surprising to see how lenient the juries are, and how light are the penalties for serious offences. The Germans and French are as little likely to tolerate a system which is unjust to innocent men as are English and Americans, and if their methods did not work well in practice, they would be changed. They are vastly more contented than are we, and the worst that happens there is not so bad as the trial of Thaw in our greatest city.

Especially does this rule operate to defeat all attempts to detect and punish the crime which at present is at once most common and most dangerous to our institutions — the crime of bribery. Since it is an offence to give as well as to take a bribe, both parties to the crime are protected from question, and as bribery is rarely committed in the presence of innocent bystanders, the criminals cannot be convicted unless they confess their guilt. In these circumstances they are as safe as the cardinals who, under the ecclesiastical law, could only be convicted of incontinence by the testimony of nine eye-witnesses. The recent disclosures as to the methods pursued in the New York legislature, the revelation of corruption in San Francisco and Pittsburg, the wholesale purchase of votes in Adams County, Ohio, the bribery attending the election of Senator Lorimer in Illinois, are only a few of many things that might be cited to show how this poison is corrupting our whole body politic. The decision of the Senate — that the votes admittedly bought in Illinois were not necessary to elect Lorimer, and that he knew nothing of the purchase though he did not take the stand before the investigating committee, shows the attitude toward such offences of men who should be, and unhappily too often are, the leaders of the community. Those who supported Lorimer in fact proceeded on the theory that the severely practical politicians of Illinois threw away money by buying unnecessary votes, and that the person most interested in the issue of a sharp conflict, himself a very practical man, was kept profoundly ignorant of what his supporters did, and they reached their conclusion when they were charged with the duty of keeping the Senate above suspicion. Such decisions make one think of Demosthenes, and wonder if our case does not resemble that of his native country when he said:

"What is it that has ruined Greece? Envy, when a man gets a bribe; laughter, if he confesses it; mercy to the convicted; hatred of those who denounce the crime, — all the usual accompaniments of corruption."

If the tide of corruption is to be stayed, we must cease to protect the criminal, we must break down the shield of silence behind which he now hides from justice. The Supreme Court of the United States has ruled that under a statute properly drawn to protect him from prosecution and punishment a man may be compelled to give evidence even though it criminates himself. We can at least pass statutes which extend this rule to cases of bribery, and at least convict half the criminals at the expense of letting the other half go, on the principle that "half a loaf is better than no bread." But why should a sensible community let half its most dangerous enemies go? We contemplate with great equanimity the prospect of destroying thousands of innocent men in war, but we shudder at the thought of asking a guilty man the questions which will prove his guilt.

A most important step towards the administration of justice will be taken when by proper changes in the Constitution and statutes the accused can be compelled to testify, and there is no good reason why we should not adopt to this extent the European procedure. We can at least try the experiment, and if it fails we can revert to our present practice. We can at least, without changing the Constitution, permit his silence when he might speak to be used as evidence of guilt. We do it now if his silence is anywhere else than in Court, for the rule is well settled that the silence of the accused, when that is said in his presence to which if innocent he would naturally reply, may be treated as evidence against him. His silence in the police station is evidence of guilt, his silence in court is nothing. The innocent man may be silent in jail from ignorance of his rights, from fear of his guardians, or perhaps from inadvertence. In court he has the judge and his counsel to protect him, and what is done is in the full light of day. If innocent he has every reason to say so. There is no chance of inattention. If then he keeps silent how absurd to ignore that silence. To every sensible man it is and must be convincing.

In court our practice is to treat the law as a game in which the defendant must be given every chance to escape, and the task of the prosecution be made as hard as possible, but except in court our practice is to treat the accused as a guilty man without rights. All over the country the method of dealing with an accused person, popularly called "the third degree," is practised without provoking any public criticism. We read that men are placed in superheated cells, that they are kept from sleeping by relays of officers who talk to them and ask them questions without ceasing; we are led to suspect other forms of torture, all employed to make the defendant criminate himself.

A recent writer in "The Nation" gives an instance which I quote from his letter:

"A young man was recently tortured by the police of one of our American cities into signing a written confession that he had poisoned his wife and six-year-old daughter. Afterwards the cause of their death was, by conclusive and unimpeached evidence . . . proved . . . to have been the inhalation of gas, given off from a defective gas water-heater. He, too, was seriously poisoned by the gas, was rendered unconscious by it, and was locked in a hospital for treatment and police surveillance. Upon gaining semiconsciousness, he was carried from his hospital bed to the municipal chamber of torture. In his weakened physical and distressed mental condition, he was subjected to such bodily violence at the hands of the police for the purpose of procuring from him this confession, that his body bore the marks of it for several weeks. He was indicted for murder solely upon that confession, which was the only evidence against him. He spent three months of his life in jail waiting for the trial by which he was not merely found not guilty, but judicially proved innocent."

LAWYER'S RESPONSIBILITIES

From another newspaper I take the following account of how a Chinaman accused of murdering a young woman was treated:

"Like a wild animal at bay, the Chinese was placed in a chair where he had to face the combined enemy. All the preparations were carried out with a methodical quietness and deliberation most calculated to wear on the nerves of a man who knows he is suspected and does not know what is in the minds of the men who are planning a combined move against him... The little Chinaman, his eyes bloodshot from exhaustion and lost sleep, was planted in a big chair while big Carey, captain of detectives, and Assistant District Attorney Theodore H. Ward stood in front of him driving their questions home... Attorney Ward, without a moment of warning, turned on the Celestial, and standing above him and pointing an accusing finger in his face, almost shouted: 'You killed Elsie Sigel.'"

"You could hear the roar of Carey's voice as he bellowed some emphatic charge, the quieter

## REFORM OF LEGAL PROCEDURE

monotone of Ward's as he prodded the Chinaman persistently, determinedly, and the falsetto squeak of Chung Sin when they stung him, as they did every now and then, to hysterical rage. . . . Police official after police official had been pecking at him all day since 6 o'clock in the morning, when Lieut. Forbes brought him down from Amsterdam, where he had been caught on Monday. . . It was not permitted to Chung Sin to sleep on Monday night. As soon as Forbes got the Chinese away from the chief at Amsterdam, he began to shoot questions at him. He grilled him while they waited for the train, while they made the long ride to this city, while they were on their way to police headquarters, and when Forbes left off Capt. Carey took it up. For twenty-four hours they racked him with questions. . . An all day's experience with the third degree at police headquarters did not shake the nerve of the Chinese. . . At one point, he began to show his annoyance at the continued questioning. He became surly and

## LAWYER'S RESPONSIBILITIES

peevish. Evidently believing a psychological moment had arrived, Captain Carey suddenly jumped up and shouted: 'You helped put the cord around the girl's neck!' Chung also jumped up, and dropped back into his chair, wheeling completely about. But it was not from fear. He had merely been startled by the noise and suddenness of the question. He insisted that he had not seen the cord around the girl's neck, and did not see the crime committed. . . . He flashed anger when Assistant District Attorney Ward and Capt. Carey tried to break him down with the constant question: 'You did tie the rope around Elsie's neck, didn't you?' Hour after hour they pounded him with that question, turning it and twisting it, but the Chinaman squirmed free every time. . . It is thought by the police that a continuation of the examination of the witness will result in his giving more valuable information."

The Chief of the Detroit detectives states his practice as follows:

## REFORM OF LEGAL PROCEDURE

"I am a police officer, not a lawyer. We've got to make laws of our own. If we suspect a man we see that he doesn't get a lawyer near him until we get through with him. We question him, and corner him up until he confesses. There was that young fellow who murdered the old woman, and who was acquitted by the jury though he confessed. We used no brutality. He said he wanted to confess, after some facts were shown to him. If a man has committed a murder, we are going to get that man to confess if we can. They break down. But, brutality, naw, none of that. Mind, I ain't saying anything about the play, but that's all wrong. We kept at Hamburger day after day. He was a well-dressed, good-looking fellow. I knew it would be hard to put it on him. But after some days he would hold his hands about his waist as if in pain, and say, 'I feel so bad. I feel so bad. I want to tell you all. But I cannot, I cannot.' We saw that we had him goin'. He finally broke down. They usually break down. And

## LAWYER'S RESPONSIBILITIES

in spite of his confession we had a hard time convicting him."

One more statement is found in the "New York World" of November 30:

"The latest thing in accommodations at the new building is what the police term the 'roast or freeze third-degree rooms.' There are two rooms in the basement to be devoted entirely to this work. They are absolutely bare and forbidding, with steel walls and pipes for quick changes of temperature. Above the grated ceilings electric lights are so arranged as to light the rooms instantly or else throw them into complete darkness. The temperature of the rooms can be lowered or increased in a few minutes, which means a real 'sweating' or a 'freeze out' for the unfortunates made to submit to the process."

These statements and others like them are made constantly in the newspapers, and one reads the nonchalant statement quite frequently that "the prisoner after undergoing the third degree confessed." Thus while we shudder at the stories of mediæval tortures and regard with horror the instruments of cruelty when we see them at Nuremberg or in other ancient fortresses, we revive them in our own cities.

In a word the Constitution jealously guards the defendant from being obliged to say anything in court where his rights would be fully protected by counsel, judge, and public opinion, but he is turned over without any protection to the mercies of police officers who, believing him guilty and goaded by the clamor of the public that the perpetrators of a crime be detected and punished, resort to all sorts of irregular and indefensible practices, carried on in the cells of jails or other places of detention, to obtain his confession of guilt. How irrational and lawless is the community which tolerates a secret inquisition by detectives and regards with horror an open inquiry in a Court! It is time that our practice was suited to the needs of justice and the changed conditions of life, and that the

## LAWYER'S RESPONSIBILITIES

accused be on the one hand protected from being obliged by secret torture to criminate himself, and on the other no longer protected against open inquiry and the proper inferences from his answers or his silence.

If we can simplify our indictments, and make the best witness testify as to the facts, it only remains to secure prompt trials with only one appeal. Grand juries should sit often enough, and trials proceed promptly upon indictment. A single appeal is enough, and in criminal as in civil cases the rule should be that only for substantial and material error should the judgment be reversed.

The grounds on which convictions are reversed are in many cases absurd. A member of the Alabama Bar addressing the Bar Association of that state said:

"I have examined about seventy-five murder cases that found their way into the reports of Alabama. More than half of these cases were reversed, and not a single one of them on any

## REFORM OF LEGAL PROCEDURE

matter that went to the merits of the case; and very few of them upon any matter that could have influenced the jury in reaching a verdict."

The same story comes from all over the country, and the American Bar Association has three times recommended the adoption of the rule that no conviction shall be set aside unless the records shows that the defendant was improperly convicted.

If the trial judge is given power to sentence immediately after verdict where in his judgment the exceptions are without merit, many foolish appeals would be discouraged and the cause of justice would not suffer. Especially is it important that judges should be slow to allow writs of error which will carry the cases of men convicted under state laws to the Supreme Court of the United States. That august tribunal may as a rule safely leave the administration of criminal justice to the tribunals of the state in which the crimes are committed, and the delays secured by appeals to the Supreme Court

are from every point of view unfortunate. For various reasons this rule should be applied less strictly to cases arising in the territories of the United States where the tribunals are apt to reflect the opinions, not of the whole population but of a certain class, and of course there must always be cases in which the interposition of the Supreme Court is necessary.

Finally a word may be said in regard to the excessive and pernicious zeal of the lawyers who defend criminals, and it is best said by President Taft:

"The conduct of the defense of criminals in this country, and the extremes to which counsel deem themselves justified in going to save their clients from the just judgment of the law, have much to do with the disgraceful condition in which we find its administration. The awakened moral conscience of the country can find no better object for its influence than in making lawyers understand that their obligation to their clients is only to see that their client's legal rights are

## REFORM OF LEGAL PROCEDURE

protected, and that they ought not to lose their identity as officers of the law in the cause of their clients and recklessly resort to every expedient to win the case. I believe that there is no escape from the evil tendencies to which I have referred, except by inducing the Bar to cleanse itself of those who in the interest of their clients forget their obligation as attorneys to the court and their duties as a citizen."

It is by such devices that the trial of Patrick Calhoun was prolonged for nearly five months in San Francisco and ended in a disagreement of the jury.

At the outset of these lectures I pointed out to you that the law and the legal profession have in late years sunk in popular estimation, and that upon you and others like you who are just entering upon practice will devolve no small part of the work which must be done to replace both in their true position. It will be your duty to make the law respected and obeyed, and to be respected it must be respectable. Judges

## LAWYER'S RESPONSIBILITIES

of high character, learning, and ability, cannot fail to command for themselves and their decisions the respect of the community, but courts alone do not make the law. We have, or shall soon have, besides the Congress of the United States some forty-eight state legislatures, and no one knows how many municipal legislatures, engaged in making laws of greater or less scope. Our people are beset with the notion that the remedy for any trouble which they encounter, however slight, is to be found in a new law, and they rush to the legislature with every sort of crude proposal for legislation. These are referred to committees more or less competent and very busy; they are hastily considered, and their consequences imperfectly appreciated. When they reach the legislature they are more hastily and inconsiderately amended, and often are passed with no adequate discussion in the closing hours of a busy session. As a result a flood of new law is let loose upon the inhabitants of each state every year or two years, and any public-spirited citizen who watches the legislature and tries to prevent foolish laws cannot but be amazed at the way in which our country is governed.

Nor is this the worst feature of the case. Our Congress and our various legislatures have it in their power to grant franchises, special privileges, and immunities. They can adjust taxation to favor some and burden others, they can pass very stringent regulations of private business like the anti-trust laws or the interstate commerce laws, or the state laws regulating the price of gas, or the relations of employer and employed. In a word they can by law put money into A's pocket and extract it from B's. Hence arises a demand from the men who want legislative aid for one set of laws, and from those who do not wish to be disturbed a pressure for other or no legislation. The danger is that the power to give a man money will not be exercised for nothing, and it is unnecessary to take your time in proving what we all know — that persons desiring to get or defeat legislation have bought and will buy legislators. The price may not be paid always in money, but in other things which men desire, such as offices, employment, chances to share in a profitable venture, or social opportunities. But whatever the price, it secures the laws which the buyer wants, and hence the jokers in tariff laws and the various questionable statutes passed in private interests, many instances of which no one familiar with state legislation can fail to recall. These influences and practices corrupt our legislation.

On the other hand the men who are so anxious to have laws passed are by no means equally anxious to obey them. The manufacturer and merchant who have secured protection by tariff legislation are found evading the very tariff laws which were passed at their instance. The recent disclosures of smuggling in New York both by wholesale importers, like The American Sugar Refining Co., and by returning travellers are too recent to need enumeration. How often do our fellow citizens who run automobiles respect the speed limit and the other regulations made to protect the public? How carefully have the railroads respected the law against rebating, — how scrupulously has the Sherman law been observed by the trusts? How carefully have the provisions of the Constitution and its requirements been respected by executive officers in our recent experience? How well have the States obeyed the Fifteenth Amendment? The prevalence of lynch law, the mob violence which attends a strike, the frauds in weights and measures discovered a year ago in New York, the departure of half the Senate of West Virginia from that state in order to secure some political advantage — all these things and many more might be cited to show that law is not respected in this country because it is law. Men prescribe new laws, and new laws, and again new laws, as a remedy for the ills of the body politic, but they despise their own medicine.

Nor is this altogether surprising. Our system

of government assumes that a statute will be passed by the representatives of the people fairly chosen, acting impartially under no improper influences, and having in mind only the public interest. When the people find that in practice this assumption is not justified; when they find trust companies slipping through the legislature a few words in a bill which exempts them from taxation; when they find a clause in a tariff which ostensibly lowers duties nullified by a "joker"; when they witness the legislative struggle between two contending corporations for a particular franchise and see how the victory is won, they lose respect for the legislators and their work. When they find them elected by fraud and their work tainted by fraud, why should they respect the laws which they make?

For some years I have spent a portion of each summer in Germany. I have gone regularly in the afternoon or evening to a garden where concerts are given daily. It is near a great city and admission is cheap. The concerts are

## REFORM OF LEGAL PROCEDURE

attended by all classes of people, and the attendance varies from six or seven hundred to more than two thousand. They sit in seats or at little tables as close as they can be put. They have anything that they want to drink. In three years I have never seen any rudeness, I have never heard a voice raised above the gentle pitch of quiet conversation, I have never seen anyone drunk, I have never seen an objectionable or disorderly person, and I have never seen a policeman. The streets in the town and neighboring country are lined with fruit trees, and no fence protects them from the public. Indeed there is hardly a fence or wall of any kind from the North Sea to Switzerland. Yet the fruit on the trees (ripe cherries of the most tempting kind) is as safe as if a dog or policeman guarded each tree. Where on this side of the water could these conditions be matched? Near what large American city are fruits and flowers safe from depredators?

On August 1, the Swiss Fourth of July, I spent

## LAWYER'S RESPONSIBILITIES

an evening on a public steamboat on the Lake of Thun which was crowded with all sorts of people. We cruised about for some hours, looking at the fireworks sent up in different places. There was a band on board and a bar, but the crowd was quiet and orderly, and a lady without an escort would have had no reason to fear any rudeness. Who would think of taking ladies on an excursion boat in the harbor of New York or Boston or any other port on the night of a holiday!

I might multiply these experiences, but I merely wish to indicate the difference between that respect for the law which seems natural to the Swiss and the Germans and which at one time was native in New England and the present conditions. It is the difference between the spirit which breathed in the Massachusetts Bill of Rights, where it is written that: "The legislature ought frequently to assemble for the redress of grievances, for correcting, strengthening, and confirming the laws and for making

## REFORM OF LEGAL PROCEDURE

new laws as the common good may require," and the feeling of to-day which dreads the assembling of any legislature, and hails its adjournment with delight. It is this feeling which leads men to do all that they can to prevent an extra session of Congress, which is content with biennial sessions of the legislature, which limits by constitution restriction the duration of the session, which fetters the power of the legislature in various ways as by preventing it from passing special laws, or insisting that each law shall deal with a single subject which must be expressed in its title.

The people's distrust of their own representatives finds expression in every recent constitution, and in the various attempts to improve municipal government by abolishing large boards of councilmen and substituting a small commission or increasing the power of a mayor.

In a sense this change in public feeling like the tendency to limit the power of judges is a reflection on our profession, for it is we who are in very large part responsible for legislation. Every legislature contains a large percentage of lawyers, and to them their associates turn for counsel on legal questions. Lawyers appear in support of or opposition to proposed laws, they argue before committees, they interview legislators, they influence legislation in open, and unhappily some times in secret ways, and as the lawyers are the professors and priests of the law in every community, so are they responsible more than any one else for bad legislation, sometimes because they procure it, and more often because through laziness, lack of public spirit, or fear of public odium they fail to oppose it. We should feel our responsibility for the laws under which our community lives, but the responsibility too often rests lightly upon our shoulders.

A statute, as I have said, should be the free and honest expression of the legislative will, and in reaching its conclusion the legislature should be kept as free from improper influence

## REFORM OF LEGAL PROCEDURE

as a judge or a jury. It is a high ideal you may say, but it is none the less the ideal to which we must aspire. There are enough influences to lower the standard. Let ours be always exerted to keep it up. In the homely phrase: "You don't hit high by aiming low."

As a legislator the lawyer should endeavor to prevent all unwise and ill-considered legislation. A change of the law should only be made after due consideration and discussion. No one can tell what mischief results when the Senate in a few hours passes bills appropriating hundreds of millions of dollars, and by the appropriation often commits the country to a mischievous policy without discussion or real consideration, as was done when the appropriation to fortify the Panama Canal was passed by the Senate without debate. The motto of the legislator should be "quality not quantity." The hasty legislation of to-day returns for correction next year, and it has been said that in Massachusetts 60 per centum of the laws passed at

one session are repealed or amended within a few years. The proportion may or may not be accurate, but a little saving of time at one session often means a great consumption of time at the next, and great mischief in the meanwhile.

Whether he sits in the legislature, or appears before its committees or in its lobbies, the lawyer should insist that no improper influence be used to influence the legislators. I cannot put the case better than I did some years ago in addressing the American Bar Association when I said that a peculiar responsibility rests upon our profession in connection with legislation: "It is we who represent great corporations before committees and conduct legislative campaigns. It is our advice upon which the representatives of great interests depend. It is to 'Legal Expenses' in corporation ledgers that many a questionable outlay has been charged. The fortune of our client may be made or destroyed by the decision of a court or the verdict of a jury. The establishment of a patent may involve as many millions as can be gained through any action of any legislature. Yet would we on that account take steps to secure a packed jury or try improperly to influence a court? The lawyer who should seek by foul means to win a verdict or secure a decision would be driven from the Bar, if discovered, and be forever disgraced. Is there any reason for regarding a legislature as less sacred than a jury? The power of the first is far greater. The interests in its charge are far more important than are often committed to a jury. The verdict affects only the parties to the cause. The law governs the whole community. Should we not on this account be even more careful to guard the legislature from improper approach?

"As officers of the court we feel bound to protect its honor. As citizens of the commonwealth are we not equally bound to defend the purity of the legislature which holds its power in sacred trust for us all, and on whose integrity rests the continued existence of the state? We know that if the community loses faith in the absolute purity of its courts, the whole social fabric is imperilled. We remember how in Cincinnati, indignant at the miscarriage of justice in court, the mob burned the Court House and did justice according to its own views. We have not forgotten how promptly the community took the law into its own hands when a jury acquitted the Italian murderers in New Orleans. In dealing with the delicate questions between labor and capital, which are pressing upon us, the legislature is the court and jury. When men's passions are as strongly enlisted as they are in these disputes, the most perfect integrity and the greatest wisdom are needed to adjust them. Absolute confidence in the arbiters is essential. Let it once be believed by the laborer that some great legislative contest has been determined against him by money, and how long will it be before we witness a riot which will be perhaps a civil war?

## REFORM OF LEGAL PROCEDURE

"The fees which are paid for very slight legislative services are large. Their size often stigmatizes the employment. The temptation is great, but we who are the interpreters and to a great extent the makers of the law, we whose consciences are educated in courts of justice, we who should lead the community up, and who know that upon respect for the law rests our whole system of government, we certainly cannot escape the gravest condemnation if, through any act, advice, or acquiescence of ours, the fountains of the law are polluted. The honor of our profession, the future of our country, are at stake. The law is in our keeping, and our hands must never weaken its hold upon the people. Let us remember the stern command of the ancient Roman, '*Tu cole justitiam. Tibi et aliis manet ultor.*'"

The phrase "corporation lawyer" has become a term of reproach, the sufficient answer of the demagogue to any argument made by the leaders of the Bar. This reproach is unjust, and its

injustice must be made apparent by our conduct. In the words of Governor Harmon the lawyer who acts for corporations: "must not forget that they unlike his ordinary clients have or may have interests which conflict with those of the public, and that his first duty is to the public, not only because he is a citizen, but because from it he has received his commission as an officer of justice."

To quote from Governor Woodrow Wilson:

"My purpose is to recall you to the service of the nation as a whole, from which you have been drifting away; to remind you that, no matter what the exactions of modern legal business, no matter what or how great the necessity for specialization in your practice of the law, you are not the servants of special interests, the more expert counsellors of this, that, or the other group of business men; but guardians of the general peace, the guides of those who seek to realize by some best accommodation the rights of men.

## REFORM OF LEGAL PROCEDURE

"You are servants of the public, of the state itself. You are under bonds to serve the general interest, the integrity and enlightenment of law itself, in the advice you give individuals. It is your duty also to advise those who make the laws — to advise them in the general interest, with a view to the amelioration of every undesirable condition that the law can reach, the removal of every obstacle to progress and fair dealing that the law can remove, the lightening of every burden the law can lift, and the righting of every wrong the law can rectify. The services of the lawyer are indispensable not only in the application of the accepted processes of the law, the interpretation of existing rules in the daily operations of life and business. His services are indispensable also in keeping and in making the law clear with regard to responsibility, to organization, to liability, and, above all, to the relation of private rights to the public interest. . .

"Some radical changes we must make in our

law and practice. Some reconstructions we must push forward which a new age and new circumstances impose upon us. But we can do it all in calm and sober fashion, like statesmen and patriots. Let us do it also like lawyers. Let us lend a hand to make the structure symmetrical, well-proportioned, solid, perfect. Let no future generation have cause to accuse us of having stood aloof, indifferent, half hostile, or of having impeded the realization of right. Let us make sure that liberty shall never repudiate us as its friends and guides. We are the servants of society, the bond-servants of justice."

Not only must we protect the legislature against corruption by citizens and their counsel, but we must protect it against the usurpation of its power by the executive. The true principle of our government is stated in the Massachusetts Bill of Rights:

"In the government of this Commonwealth, the legislative department shall never exercise the executive and judicial powers, or either of

## REFORM OF LEGAL PROCEDURE

them; the executive shall never exercise the legislative and judicial powers, or either of them; the judicial shall never exercise the legislative and executive powers, or either of them; to the end it may be a government of laws and not of men."

The people through their representatives chosen for that purpose make the laws.

The executive officers, president or governor, are chosen to execute the laws. They have the power to suggest laws which they think wise, and to veto those which they think unwise, but no more. The power to recommend is not the power to legislate. Whatever influence can be exerted by recommendation, the executive has the right to exercise, but no more. Some body of men must decide what legislation is wise, and the legislature is that body of men. The President may have one opinion as to what law should be passed, the Supreme Bench another, the House of Bishops perhaps a third, but the legislature's judgment must prevail.

LAWYER'S RESPONSIBILITIES

The Governor or the President may explain to the people why he advises a certain measure as President Lincoln used to do, and as Governor Hughes recently did in New York, but when he goes beyond this limit, when he gives or withholds patronage to influence votes, he is in fact bribing the legislature. The offices are created in order that the public business may be done, not to provide a corruption fund, and when appointments are made or refused to secure support for the executive's policy, when members of the legislature are rewarded or punished not for voting as they think right but for voting as the executive wishes, they are influenced corruptly, and the will of the executive not the judgment of the legislature makes the law.

The question is not whether a given measure is good or bad; if bad it should not be passed, if good public opinion can be trusted eventually to force its passage. The question is who shall decide whether it is good or bad, the executive or the legislature, and whether the decision when made shall be the honest judgment of the legislator, or simply a decision which he is paid to render by getting something that he wants for himself.

The tendency to control the legislature by other means than fair argument has of late been unpleasantly manifest. "My policy," as President Johnson called it, or "my policies," the phrase adopted by his recent successors, are phrases of ill omen, and it is the duty of our profession to resist all efforts to impose upon the representatives of the people the policies or opinions of one man by any appeal to improper motives. And I say this though I favor many of the measures which are thus improperly pressed. What is done to-day for good ends is a precedent which may be quoted hereafter, when the same things are done to promote bad measures. The public opinion of the American people is the only weapon that a President needs to carry any good measure through Congress. When that fails, the measure should fail too.

## LAWYER'S RESPONSIBILITIES

And now, gentlemen, my task is done. You are about to enter the service of the law, and perhaps are familiar with the sonorous words in which Hooker describes the ideal law:

"Her seat is the bosom of God, her voice the harmony of the world, all things in Heaven and Earth do her homage, the very least as feeling her care, and the greatest as not exempted from her power."

It is this ideal for which you must labor, and the rewards which await him who shall do his part in lifting our profession from its present low estate, in making the administration of the law a prompt and efficient method of doing justice, and in causing the law everywhere to be respected and worthy of respect are far greater than any fortune or fame which he, however brilliant he may be, can hope to win, who makes himself only the tool of his client. The unscrupulous lawyer who sells his talents and espouses any cause or adopts any means to accomplish his client's ends, who makes his client in a word his master, will live to say with Wolsey, and with as bitter regret:

"Had I but served my God with half the zeal I served my king, he would not in mine age have left me naked to mine enemies."

# INDEX

Accused, The, value of testimony of, 215-6; advantage of direct interrogation of, 222

Accident Insurance, report of New York Commission on, 57; the problem of, 61; certain systems of, 63; fraternal method, 65; advantage of Mutual Fire Insurance, illustrated, 66; premium for, explained, 68; possible advantage of State participation in, 70, 71; German system of, 75, 77; report of the Committee on the Judiciary of the National House of Representatives on, 78; President Roosevelt on, 80; railroad and steamboat and railroad passengers and, 82-3

"Advance" of Chicago on crime, 198-9

Alabama Bar, address of member of, 231-2

Alger, George W., article by, quoted from, 104-8

American Bar Association, recommendation of to Congress, 171; recommendation of on setting aside of convictions, 232; author's address before, 245-7

Appeals, Court of, quoted on changing testimony, 106; cause of delay in, 170

Arizona, new constitution of, 7

Bar Association of New York, report of committee, 146-7

Bartlett, Sydney, advice of Mr. Justice Miller to, 163

Biglow, Hosea, aphorism quoted, 160

Borough, President, case of, 145-6

Boston, frequency of personal injury suits in, 51; cost of

# INDEX

jury sessions in, 56; comparative infrequency of disagreements in, 191
Bowen, Lord Justice, quoted, 148
Bribery, recent disclosures as to methods, 219
Brougham, Lord, quoted on duty to client, 29, 30
Brown, Mr. Justice, on a recent statute, 119-20

Calhoun, Patrick, prolongation of trial of, 234
Clifford, Mr. Justice, quoted, 157
Courts, what the decisions of decide, 24; rules of English, 36; partially responsible for existing abuses, 125; advantages of hearing before, 135-6; plans adopted for securing speed in English, 142-4; plea for establishment of final judges, 149; point of view of, 162; advantages of oral argument in, 163-5; need for increased power of, 173; criminals nowadays protected by, 217
Crippen Case, time taken to select jury in, 211; publisher fined for false statement concerning, 213
Cross-examination, a dangerous amusement, 96; rules for, 97

Delay, causes during trial, 92; remedies for, 93; in Philadelphia v. Pittsburgh, 108-9; how to avoid, 109; reading judgments, cause of, 170
Demosthenes, cited, 220
Dickinson, Secretary, quoted, 201
Disputed Wills, source of litigation, 89; method of avoiding, 89, 90
"Dooley, Mr.," on judges, 165-6; on the convict's chances, 217

Eliot, President, quoted, 199
*Ellis* v. *Delaware, Lackawanna and Western R. R. Co.*, 105
Employers' Liability, President Roosevelt on, 80

# INDEX

England, procedure in, 48; description of court in, 98; place of Judge in, 111; on Judges summing up in, 123; counsel not limited in 161; work of Judges in, in comparison with Chicago, Massachusetts, 187–90; jury easily impanelled in, 211

Folk, Governor, effect of imperfect indictment in convictions secured by, 209; conspicuous rascal on convictions of, 209
France, system of interrogation of witnesses in, 218
Franchise Tax Law, case of, 146

Germany, on direct interrogation of accused in, 218; author's experience in, 239–40; respect for law in, 241

Hamilton, Alexander, quoted, 174
*Harbin* v. *Masterman*, L. R. 1st Chan. Div., 37
Hoar, Judge, on beginning opinion, 168
Holt, Judge, on number of criminals, 195
Hopkins, Charles T., on Atlanta riots, quoted, 201
Hooker, description of the ideal law, 255
Hough, Judge, statement of, 130–2
Hughes, Mr. Justice, quoted, 159
Humphreys, Judge, censured, 6

Indictment, its object, 203; suggested form of, 204; so-called flaws of, 205; examples of imperfect, 206–8; instances of results of, 209; need of simple forms of, 210
Interstate Commerce Act, subject of study in law courts, 19

Jeffrey, Lord, quoted, 12
Judges, described as "fossilized," "reactionary," 6; dictum

## INDEX

of English, 54; duties of, in relation to altercations between counsel, 93; duties in cross-examination, 94; story of an English, 94-5; charge of a, 101; slight chance of injustice from error of, 103; capacity of, 110; status in England of, 111; Mr. Justice Gray on, 112; Mr. Justice Brewer on, 113; powers and limitations of, 114; need for, 115; Professor Pound on, 116; further limitations of, 117; full powers of, instanced, 121; character of, 168; need for strong men as, 169; political structure resting on power of, 174; need of strong bench of, 175-6; how to be obtained, 177; should be adequately rewarded, 179; difficulty of securing, 180-1; restraint of political burden, 181; inadequate treatment of, 183; quotation from a Kentucky, 184; cost of increased salaries of, 185; selection of, in comparison with England, 186-7; number of in Massachusetts, 187; in further comparison with England, 188-90; no greater number of, required, 190; charge of able Massachusetts, 214; saying of another, 215

Jury, imperfect consideration of, 99; story of a member of, 101; province of, 102; system for, 102-3; desirability of furnishing stenographer's report, to, 122-3; delay in securing, 209-10; able judge's charge to, Massachusetts, 214

Law, respect for essential, 2; is civilization, 11; on the reforms in, 13-15; drawn hastily, 18; the delay of, 21-3, 5; value of delay of, 26-8; cause for delay of, 32; different systems of the, U. S., 150; need for uniformity of, 151-3; obedience to, illustrated, 214; how freshly created, 235; how adversely affected by legislation, 236-7; power of legislation in regard to, 252

Lawsuit, defined, 27; severe competitive examination of, 42; settlement of, delayed for six years, 44; prolific

# INDEX

cause of delay of, 46; real estate and insurance, less frequent cause of, 50-1

Lawyers, duty of, leaders of community in past, 2; serious faults of, 6; incapable as leaders, 9; as American statesmen, 10; champions of liberty, 11; Massachusetts, form of oath of, 30; San Francisco Bar on duties of, 31; ethics of, 32; standards for, 38; need of keener professional conscience of, 46; remark of a, 46; need for association of, 86; fear of tricky, 87; address to jury of, unlimited in Iowa and North Carolina, 117; power of, in Texas, 118; obligation of, to aid court, 157; true attitude of, instanced, 158; responsible for legislation, 243; duties of, as legislators, 244

Lincoln, Abraham, cited, 1; "an honest lawyer," 40; a biographical note of, 41

London, few homicides in, during 1909, 195

Lorimer, Senator, decision of Senate in regard to, 220

Louisville, Kentucky, number of homicides in, 197

Lowell, Judge John, the late, rule of, 167

Master or Referee, class of cases held before, 124; hearing before occasion of delay, 125; nominal power of, 128; prolific sources of delay, causes for, 134; system of, unsound, 139; suggested remedies for, 140-1

Massachusetts, collection of debts in, 34; quotation from commission appointed in, 47; Bill of Rights of, quoted from, 183; number of judges in, 187; population of in relation to judiciary, 188; comparison with England, 188-9; Bill of Rights quoted from, 241-51

Mexican, Law, covering Accident Insurance, 72

Miller, Mr. Justice, advice of, quoted, 163

Miller, Tax Assessor, marvelous letter of; 202

"Nation, The," a letter to, quoted, 223-4

National Economic League, Council of, vote of, 8

# INDEX

Nebraska, Supreme Court of, provision in Constitution, how affecting, 119

Newspapers, full narratives of crime appear in, 211; abuse of, an impediment to justice, 213

"New York World," statement from, 229

O'Gorman, Justice, quoted, 147

Personal Injury Suits, nature of, frequency of, 51-3; abuse of medical testimony in, 54-5; reduction of damages in, 59; speech of a lawyer in, 100

Roosevelt, Theodore, cited, 1; on public leaders, 9; Harvard Alumni address quoted, 17; address at Jamestown on accident liability, 80

Scoville, Mr., on delay of jury trial in Philadelphia, 108

Sherman, Anti-trust Law, varying interpretations of, 154

Sumner, Charles, saying of, 39

Supreme Court, rights of poor man in, 4; campaign upon, 6; on the Sherman law, 18; in Nebraska, 119; right to invoke should be rendered easy, 155; on appeals to, 232

Taft, William Howard, as a judicial authority, 2; Chicago speech quoted, 3; on defense of criminals, 233

Taxes, numerous and ill-assorted, 152; instance of unfairness of, 153

Third Degree, the, 223; instances of, 224-5; chief of Detroit detectives, method of, 228; mediæval torture of, 230; illogical attitude of public towards, 230-1

Tichborne Case, claimant, length of trial of, 25; charge of Chief Justice Cockburn in, 111-2

# INDEX

"Times," of London, article from, quoted, 109
"Tribune," Chicago, figures on homicides, quoted, 195

Untermeyer, Samuel, suggestion of, 88

Vance, Professor, on the American Lawyer, 5

*Whitcomb* v. *Converse*, cited, 158
White, Andrew D., President, quoted, 196; "New Bedford Standard" on, 196–7
Wilson, Woodrow, Governor, quoted, 249–50
Witnesses, trials of, 126–7


THE·PLIMPTON·PRESS·NORWOOD·MASS·U·S·A

Trieste Publishing has a massive catalogue of classic book titles. Our aim is to provide readers with the highest quality reproductions of fiction and non-fiction literature that has stood the test of time. The many thousands of books in our collection have been sourced from libraries and private collections around the world.

The titles that Trieste Publishing has chosen to be part of the collection have been scanned to simulate the original. Our readers see the books the same way that their first readers did decades or a hundred or more years ago. Books from that period are often spoiled by imperfections that did not exist in the original. Imperfections could be in the form of blurred text, photographs, or missing pages. It is highly unlikely that this would occur with one of our books. Our extensive quality control ensures that the readers of Trieste Publishing's books will be delighted with their purchase. Our staff has thoroughly reviewed every page of all the books in the collection, repairing, or if necessary, rejecting titles that are not of the highest quality. This process ensures that the reader of one of Trieste Publishing's titles receives a volume that faithfully reproduces the original, and to the maximum degree possible, gives them the experience of owning the original work.

We pride ourselves on not only creating a pathway to an extensive reservoir of books of the finest quality, but also providing value to every one of our readers. Generally, Trieste books are purchased singly - on demand, however they may also be purchased in bulk. Readers interested in bulk purchases are invited to contact us directly to enquire about our tailored bulk rates. Email: customerservice@triestepublishing.com

# You May Also Like

**Geological Survey of Missouri: A Preliminary Report on the Coal Deposits of Missouri from Field Work Prosecuted During the Years 1890 and 1891**

**Arthur Winslow**

ISBN: 9780649691807
Paperback: 244 pages
Dimensions: 6.14 x 0.51 x 9.21 inches
Language: eng

**War Poems, 1898**

**California Club & Irving M. Scott**

ISBN: 9780649731213
Paperback: 160 pages
Dimensions: 6.14 x 0.34 x 9.21 inches
Language: eng

www.triestepublishing.com

# You May Also Like

ISBN: 9780649690602
Paperback: 114 pages
Dimensions: 6.14 x 0.24 x 9.21 inches
Language: eng

**Reports of the Board of Directors and of the Superintendents of the State Hospitals for the Insane at Raleigh, Goldsboro and Morganton, North Carolina**

## State Hospital of North Carolina

ISBN: 9780649066155
Paperback: 144 pages
Dimensions: 6.14 x 0.31 x 9.21 inches
Language: eng

**Heath's Modern Language Series. Atala**

## François-René de Chateaubriand & Oscar Kuhns

www.triestepublishing.com

# You May Also Like

## Report of the Department of Farms and Markets, pp. 5-71

### Various

ISBN: 9780649333158
Paperback: 84 pages
Dimensions: 6.14 x 0.17 x 9.21 inches
Language: eng

## Catalogue of the Episcopal Theological School in Cambridge Massachusetts, 1891-1892

### Various

ISBN: 9780649324132
Paperback: 78 pages
Dimensions: 6.14 x 0.16 x 9.21 inches
Language: eng

www.triestepublishing.com

# You May Also Like

ISBN: 9780649352142
Paperback: 88 pages
Dimensions: 6.14 x 0.18 x 9.21 inches
Language: eng

# Three Hundred Tested Recipes

## Various

ISBN: 9780649419418
Paperback: 108 pages
Dimensions: 6.14 x 0.22 x 9.21 inches
Language: eng

# A Basket of Fragments

## Anonymous

Find more of our titles on our website. We have a selection of thousands of titles that will interest you. Please visit

www.triestepublishing.com

Lightning Source UK Ltd.
Milton Keynes UK
UKOW01f1326231017
311488UK00017B/3743/P